Leading like a Professional
From the Trenches to the Executive Floor
Thomas Gast

AF199336

"A true leader has the confidence to stand alone, the courage to make tough decisions, and the compassion to listen to the needs of others. He does not set out to be a leader, but becomes one by the equality of his actions and the integrity of his intent."
(Douglas MacArthur)

Author's Bio

In February 1985, Thomas Gast joined the French Foreign Legion. Upon completion of his basic training, he was deployed to the Jungle Regiment in French Guiana (3rd Foreign Infantry Regiment). In September 1987, aided by a German legionnaire officer, he managed to get into the only para regiment of the Foreign Legion (2nd REP). He rose through the ranks, soon made sergeant and finally, after barely 11 years, he became a platoon leader and company sergeant major. After his service in the Legion, Thomas Gast spent a long time in security. He lived and worked in Saudi Arabia: as security staff. Client: Delegation of the European Commission at Riyadh. Haiti: as country manager, (CEO). Client: Delegation of the European Commission at Pétionville. Israel: as deputy country manager at the European Commission Technical Assistance Office, (ECTAO). Yemen: as security team leader, acting for a French company. Client: The Yemen Liquefied Natural Gas Project, (YLNG). Red Sea, Gulf of Aden, Arabian Sea, since 2004 to date: on behalf of a renowned British company, the author guards British vessels against pirate attacks as privately contracted armed security personnel (PCASP). His book 'PRIVATE SECURITY' is well and widely received amongst the security branches.

Bibliographic information of the German National Library: The German National Library lists this publication in the German National Bibliography; detailed bibliographic data are available on the internet- http://dnb.dnb.de

Impressum
© 2018 Thomas Gast. Author.

Richthofenhöhe 30

95445 Bayreuth

thomaslegion@rocketmail.com

ISBN: 9783748100973

Herstellung und Verlag:

BoD- Books on Demand, Norderstedt

A NOTE TO THE READER

This book first appeared on October 10, 2011 under the title "Ways to Success: Successful Staff Leadership – In a different Way" (German edition). Meanwhile endowed with a new title, a more sophisticated text, a clearer structure as well as additional examples taken from practice, the work is back on the book market. To the discerning reader, this overall enhanced publication offers detailed insights into the world of leadership and the world of the executive floor. Review by Moro, July 7, 2012:

"I have been leading employees for 20 years, and I have attended numerous, partly "ultra-expensive" leadership seminars. It was more out of curiosity that I bought the book "Ways to Success" – and I am all enthusiastic about it. It is written in a no-frills style, and it provides the answers to all the prerequisites that make a good boss. No matter if it's sensitive or "tough" co-workers, whether it's known troublemakers or the run-of-the-mill daily routine – the book by Thomas Gast, or better: his views on leadership, will equally apply to all of the above. In brief, I am ecstatic. The book is better than all the dear seminars and seminar materials put together, since it precisely summarizes the essentials. It is exactly as the author describes it, and nothing else.

No matter what some top-coach wants to make you believe (never leading "obnoxious" people himself), no matter what "elaborate" Q&A-techniques they sell you as good leadership – so far, none of them has been able to match Thomas Gast. Thanks, I would purchase it all over again." (Original review in German).

WHO IS THE READER?

This book addresses all bosses, training managers, team leaders, military cadres, department heads, supervisors and all those who aspire to such a position. I will refrain from giving you advice on how to achieve a role as cadre. But I do wish to support you in keeping your position for as long as humanly possible. Your success is important to me!

Meeting with success?

There is no secret formula for success; yet if you shortly bear with my real-life examples, study them meticulously and put the lessons learned to excellent use in your real job life, you are closer to the truth (and success) than you might imagine. One thing, however, should be crystal clear to the reader. I do not feel it is my vocation to show bosses in middle or upper management positions how their job works. That is why I deliberately leave out 'management' as such.

You live in a city? Good! Open the window and cast a glance outside. Out in the streets, behind closed windows, in jammed factory halls, cold offices and corporate buildings as well as in abominable supermarkets, there is a hustle and bustle of an exorbitant number of people who call themselves "boss" – and they are only happy when they can micromanage or administer everything to death. Most of them have only one ambition: Their own stable job! With their sights firmly locked on a lifelong stipend, the pension, the appreciation by a superior and their own prestige, they will always run amok when overtaken by another person or whenever their own success (or the aforementioned appreciation) fails to happen. This total aspiration towards security and status is not only boring, it is simply wrong. At least when the environment 'colleagues, co-workers and employees' is suffering as a consequence, when their own integrity goes overboard, and when one is forced to literally climb over heaps of corpses in order to approach the defined target.

This book is meant to help do things differently, but: What I am writing is no science. What I put down on paper is not the result of research, statistics or the findings of obscure studies, since I hold no qualification in any of these domains. I want to pit my hands-on experience against all of this. My experience in terms of leadership. You are going to find out pretty quickly that the pages you are reading here are testament to exceptional success stories. The real-life examples took place exactly as I describe them here. Of course, they are neither ordinary nor everyday occurrences. Which supervisor in Europe is compelled to put a handgun in his drawer – for fear of reprisals or sheer agony – when s/he has to conduct a 'cumbersome' staff appraisal? I know of no-one. But it has happened to me. In Haiti, to give the place a name. I am using this example right at the beginning. It is destined to teach the boss (you) a lesson. At the very least, it should entice him (you) to think. To get him to ask himself that question: How would I, as a superior, respond when exposed to such a situation, here translated into a European setting? All the other examples can easily be transferred one-to-one: to the firm; to the company; to the enterprise or to the company (mil.). To pretty much everything, provided you have the gift to read between the lines. In addition, I would like to show you how to push people into the abyss, and how wonderful the free fall can be for those concerned. I wish to prove to you that it is possible to push everybody's boundaries; these boundaries may also deliberately and voluntarily be pushed by the individual concerned. What I aim at is presenting to you a highly unconventional kind of leadership. My first and foremost message to all executives is: Prove to the staff in your company:

That they are strong.

That nothing is impossible.

That they have their place.

That they are significant.

That it is possible for work to be fun.

The second message goes out to you, you leaders: Lead in a way you want to be led yourself, but do not forget that there is a higher goal than to make all personnel happy at all cost: Joint success!

HOW THE BOOK CAME ABOUT

In February 2000, my first book was published. *The Legion – With the 2nd REP to the hot spots of this world* (original title in German). It was both non-fiction and autobiography. Its success was mediocre, but still; the volume received excellent reviews. From a literary point of view, I thereby found myself in the lower 12.5 pc of the ranking of German authors, in a gray zone that required more than just an autobiography to get out of. Yet, writing was my passion. And I wanted to serve that passion, no matter what the cost. Analyzing the merely modest success, I pondered what I might do better in the future. In my view, the book was tainted with an unforgivable flaw. The Delphic point seemed to be the subject itself. When scrutinizing the German book market, I soon realized that people are prone to spend much more money on a cookbook with summer dishes from Provence or on a self-help book on parenting than on the autobiography of a man who had served seventeen years in the French Foreign Legion. At some point, however, the tide turned. Print runs of my book went through the roof as the renowned author and sports journalist Carsten Germann crossed my path. In its 20/12 edition, FOCUS-magazine suddenly described the book as *simply the standard work of reference on the Foreign Legion*. Editors and publishers virtually stampeded through my door. They wanted more, wanted to see blood, chicanery and heaps of corpses, they wanted all that is called cliché and triviality. A reputable Munich publishing house thought themselves appointed to play to exactly that cliché till the cows come home. One day, there was a knock on my door, in the shape of a ghostwriter. The publishing house was well known for best marketing any of its books in print, with no venues nor vehicles of distribution barred: TV-interviews. YouTube. Commentaries and articles in the biggest daily newspapers, etc. They promised me 250,000 copies sold for the first year. Wow. It had a certain ring to it. I thought about it for a moment, and I declined the publisher's offer. Why? Well, I was a stickler for the truth. I categorically objected to the telling of lies in order to make myself look better or to earn more money. Moreover, my text was sacrosanct to me. The day I give up the monopoly on my texts, leave it to a ghostwriter, I cease to be an author and writer. But back to Carsten Germann. The article that resulted from our encounter appeared in *Welt am Sonntag* on July 17, 2011 (circulation: 440,000; coverage: 1,200,000 readers), and the week after already saw my mailbox filled with requests, proposals and suggestions. One of the weirdest ideas, as I thought at first, came from a dear friend, the director of a booming enterprise.

Another was courtesy of the training manager of a notable Swiss automobile group. They both asked me to lend an ear to a cause that they cherished a lot. They wanted me to furnish, free of charge, the key to an enhanced, successful leadership style to their respective echelons of leaders, which – as I gathered between the lines – were frustrated and at times at a loss.

1. **How do you lead?**

2. **How does one motivate?**

3. **What do I have to do so that my personal leadership style has a sustainably positive effect on the staff's motivation (employees); that the efficiency of every single one of them (provided there is sound management on the upper levels) comes to bear on harmony, productivity and the corporate image, long-term effects desired?**

The questions that were put to me were at times very elaborate, which actually caught me by surprise. Here they are.

- *How do you lead in the Foreign Legion?*

- *How do you experience the subject of leadership in a situation of crisis?*

- ***How is the Foreign Legion organized?***

- ***What did you experience there?***

If we substitute the above bullet points so that they are fit for civil application, we might arrive at the following.

- ***What (personal/in-house) leadership do I choose?***

- ***How do I lead under stress, under pressure, amidst chaos?***

- ***How do I structure my department and what are my experiences?***

- ***What feedback, what testimonials are of interest?***

But stop! I believe, I owe the reader an explanation at first, detailing why, for what reason and through which profound legitimization it is the Foreign Legion, of all organizations, that serves as a kind of role model here, and how I personally fit the bill. Let me digress for a moment. The Foreign Legion is a unit (enterprise / firm / corporation) that wholly consists of volunteers. These volunteers belong to different races and religions. They hail from 135 different countries (language – or communication issues). They represent all age groups (from 17 to retirement age) as well as all walks of life. Among them you will find:

the engineer from Reykjavík; the hooligan from Manchester; the prince from the country of Georgia; the guru from Nepal; the parson from the French province; the loser; the winner; the hunter and the hunted. You can well imagine that, in order to lump everybody together, one needs strong leaders. And these leaders will have to be led by people who are extremely familiar with 'worldwide leadership ethics'. Here, no diploma will suffice, no coaching, no truism. What is needed is an exemplary, competent and strong leadership concept; otherwise you could never master all the problems resulting from the diversity, the heterogeneity and the background of the employees. I certainly do not exaggerate when I boldly assert that what is called 'globalization' was a topic in the Legion at a time when most European businesses would ignore the very meaning of the term. Oh my god, did I really mention problems / issues earlier on in the text? Well, there are none! The Legion is successful. It is the most powerful army corps (corporation / company / enterprise) in the world. It is unique as it is self-confident and efficient (image / turnover / profit). It is at the vanguard, and hence an example to emulate, of integration (accomplished, multicultural personnel management whilst using the broad gamut of individual skills). Meanwhile, there are about a dozen other armies (companies / enterprises / corporations) that look to the 'Foreign Legion Model' for guidance. We need no longer rack our brains about the 'why': The echelon of leaders in the Legion makes the impossible possible! The Legion shop operates effectively, from one success to the next. Like a well-oiled machinery. It is running 'colorfully' and smoothly.

So what is my role in all of this?

I was part of that echelon of leaders in the Foreign Legion. From December 1989 to 1991 I was squad leader (read: head of department); then, until 1995, deputy platoon commander and from 1995 to 1997 platoon leader (read: full-time manager with 45 employees). In 1997 I achieved the great feat. I was deployed to HQ, and my office was on the same floor, just three doors down from that of the regimental commander (director general / CEO). From now on it was my task to train the instructors.

To train the instructors!

Do you notice something?

I no longer instructed legionnaires (workers or employees), but their instructors: the bosses! All of a sudden I was a practical instructor of bosses!

Among other things I was the person responsible for the entire section of simulation, ammunition, shooting ranges, shooting- and firearms instruction, and all of that for a regiment (corporation / company / enterprise) of more than 1,200 men. In the year

2008, now in the civil sector, I was trusted with the management of 145 civilians. A little later: same story. Only this time in Israel. In respect of those latter two tasks, I benefited directly from my experience in the Foreign Legion. Everything can be converted, and therefore, I would like to see you partake in this efficient way *to lead* throughout the following chapters. To let you participate in a concept that makes sense, and which is bound to meet with success in due course.

A PRINCIPLE OF COINCIDENCE?

It certainly is a coincidence that Philip Rosenthal at first served in the Foreign Legion before he went on to have great success elsewhere. He was CEO of the factory that bears his name, an enterprise with over 10,000 employees, prior to becoming a member of the German parliament for the Social Democrats (SPD).

It certainly is a coincidence too that Simon Murray (Commander of the British Empire) at first served in the Foreign Legion before turning into one of the most successful managers and businessmen of his time. (From 1994 until 1998 he was CEO of the Deutsche Bank Group in Asia as well as CEO of GEMS and GLENCORE. In the 1980s and 90s he was called the "Tai Pan" of Hong Kong, and he was the oldest man to reach the South Pole without assistance at the age of 63.

Simply attributable to coincidence is also the fact that Dominique Vandenberg served five years in the ranks of the Foreign Legion before successfully pursuing a career as an actor, stunt choreographer and author in Hollywood, starring in movies like Gangs of New York together with Leonardo DiCaprio and Cameron Diaz.

Coincidence did of course play a part when Hans Hartung (artist of international standing, e.g. extraordinary member of the Academy of Arts in Berlin. In 1960, Hartung is awarded the International Grand Prix for Painting, and he is an Oskar-Kokoschka laureate) became truly famous after serving in the Foreign Legion.

The same principle of coincidence applies to Ernst Jünger and so many other former legionnaires.

Their accidental, common denominator?

Legion – Success!

Now, I'm having the problem that I don't believe in coincidence. (The author).

A ROBUST REAL-LIFE EXAMPLE FOR STARTERS

Haiti, Pétionville. September 2008. In my capacity as Country Manager of a British company, I had to take a difficult decision: to fire one of my security guards! The man had caused some attention by either not showing up for work or being always late. He hated his job, he ignored admonitions. Talking to his supervisor about this matter seemed to bore him. When I personally found him asleep on duty, the time had come to do something about it, as he was clearly undermining troop morale, to use the military term here. Before I could summon him to my office in order to serve him a dismissal without notice, my deputy Baptiste knocked on my door. He told me that our candidate had got wind of his dismissal and that he wasn't happy about it, which in itself did not yet pose a serious problem. However, according to Baptiste, the guy had been a member of the former president Duvalier's (a.k.a. Baby Doc) death squads some years before. Baby Doc, a.k.a. Jean-Claude Duvalier reigned over Haiti from 1971 to 1986 as a dictatorial president. Under his and his father's regime, an estimated 60,000 people were brutally tortured and executed. Even in 2008, Haiti was expecting the return of the death squads' founder. As former commander of the PNH (Haitian national police, law enforcement authority) Baptiste had gained this information from a totally reliable source. So, our man was a dangerous headhunter who had already, and in cold blood, dispatched well over a dozen people to kingdom come. Baptiste strongly advised me against seeing the guy in my office without backup, since 'the candidate' was said to always carry a weapon. "If he sees a chance to kill you today, he will", Baptiste said ominously. I decided not to give him this very chance. During the talk, Baptiste should stay with me in my office. In the semi-open drawer to my right, I would keep a pistol which I could get out within a second and aim at the guy. Baptiste would do likewise; his desk was three meters to my right. I was being serious. Should an armed confrontation happen, my act would be a case of classic self-defense. I was a man with a huge sense of fairness, but honesty made no sense at that point. Not in a country where a man's demise hardly warranted three lines in the local press. When the candidate entered the office and saw our determined faces, he grasped the situation immediately; he knew what was at stake. He knew we wouldn't be pussyfooting around or indulge in endless talking. Within two seconds he had gauged his chances, he finally cracked a bitter smile and said: "You have won". He signed his dismissal in silence. We never saw him again. Double caution was called for, however, since to him I was solely responsible for his dismissal.

"He is going to catch you on your own!"

Baptiste made no bones about his analysis.

And myself? I was forewarned!

A few pages later, I will list the properties a boss should possess. There is talk of intelligence. But also of feeling. And moral fiber. I'll broach these in a bit, but for now let us go back to the situation.

What had happened?

Our man had broken all the rules. Needless to say that his colleagues were keeping an eye on his antics, for they also knew about his grim past. There even was some betting. They all wagered that nobody in their right mind would have the guts to fire that man.

They were wrong. My intelligence (head) and feeling (heart) aside, I had demonstrated moral fiber (resolve). If I hadn't, the respect for me would have melted like snow in Sahara. In order to pull the strings, I had risked my life. In the period following this episode I filled the executive chair better than ever. The "directeur", as I was called, was a wise man one could confidently look up to. Conclusion: You are fully entitled to see conflicts as chances. I had shown severity, not lost my dignity, and I had not trampled on the employee's dignity either. I had neither made the attempt to change him nor to educate him; instead, I had been looking for – and found – the best solution for both parties (company / employee). We were not happy to have him, he was not particularly happy having to work at all.

DONE EVERYTHING RIGHT?

In the years between 2003 and 2014 I traveled three continents on security missions. Looking back on that closed chapter now, I can't help but perceive two prevalent things. First, there is the fact that for people like me, there actually are adventures, even after the Legion, that warrant packing one's suitcases. It was not primarily for the money, but for the old demons beckoning to me. To soothe them was my duty and, I admit, a pleasure too. I had learned one more language and seen countries that I had only known by the proverbial finger on the map. I had made friends, yet again. That's what counts. The second, and probably the most important realization was that after all those years I could still look at myself in the mirror and say: Yes! I have done everything right.

Done everything right?

I am afraid only very few people do. Once a boss arrives at this conclusion, he can put a little crown on his head. But what makes a good boss after all? What properties, values and qualities must, or should he possess? I'll try and answer this question in four tiny paragraphs.

The boss …

"… is a guarantor of success. One who fights against gradually growing routine, for the "treadmill routine" is the death of every good act, and the decline of any endeavor for novelty. All the while, he is not about revolutionizing time-proven systems and processes. The target to be reached is set by the management. The boss below, and his cadres, fix the stages leading up to this target. The good boss inspires the employees with motivation along that road. He strives for new ideas and improvements, but he remains loyal to the company philosophy and existing corporate culture."

The boss …

"… preserves and maintains the cult of being well informed all the time. Informed about everything regarding his and the superordinate department. He masters his environment and he anticipates; hence, he hardly ever is entirely taken by surprise by anything. His fundamental quality, however, is to hold the reins on his level. Sometimes taut, sometimes lax, he pulls the strings. He always comes up with a solution to the respective potential issues. He 'considers' doing this or that … before it is too late. He is there when you need him!"

The boss …

"… is modest! The cadre, the employees and coworkers are watching him. The 'new one'. The boss. They dally with his weaknesses, his shortcomings, the lack of rigor in him, his debauchery, his potential demagogy and his arrogance. Modesty is therefore his duty."

The boss …

"… has the gift not to categorically brush off sound advice – dished out by superiors as well as by his peers or subordinates. As a superior, never shy away from asking employees (other cadres) their opinion. Above all, when there are impending innovations or novel projects. To involve employees gives you space and time to detect your own fallacies. The process of involvement and listening makes the boss grow."

Care for an example of the latter from the Legion? So be it! My platoon leader in French Guiana was a fledgling lieutenant, a rookie to the regiment. He was fresh from the OCS (Military Academy of Saint-Cyr). This brilliant officer was sturdy, in perfect physical shape, he wore spectacles, and he did not make the mistake so often made by other lieutenants before him, to look down upon us and to studiously ignore the voice of his deputy. He simply was too intelligent for that. His platoon sergeant, a so-called sous-officier adjoint, was a Hungarian with the rank of a sergent-chef, and an old warhorse. As such, one of his many tasks was to take the lieutenant under his wings, "to bring him into line". This is an indispensable process in the Legion, since an officer knows nothing of those *men without name*. Most officers will crash-land, if they do not listen to their deputies, the old legionnaires, once in a while. Absurd officer pride is totally uncalled for.

What do we make of this?

Listen; fetch advice, if in doubt. Gathering your confidantes around you to discuss something together is not a weakness. On the contrary: it is a sign of greatness.

HEAD, HEART AND BALLS

The following event took place in Calvi (Corsica), in the NCOs' mess, in 1995. A celebration was due. 'Bright eyed and bushy tailed', clad in uniforms whose knife-edge ironed creases would have cut your skin, we were a happy crowd, eating fish, runner beans and roast potatoes. And we were drinking good wine. Our attention was entirely directed on our visitor, Johann Wallisch. He, unlike us, was wearing civil clothes. And he was entitled to do so, having abandoned his uniform many years before. Wallisch was an example to us all, and a boss. Born in Upper Austria in 1926, fate had turned him into a soldier at an early age. As a member of the German paratroopers, he once fought in Normandy. He was one of the survivors of the Falaise Pocket, and he fought with distinction in the Battle of Arnhem. His next port of call was imprisonment and escape. Captured by the Americans and handed over to the French, he joined the Foreign Legion in 1945. As a legionnaire, he first served in the 3rd Foreign Infantry Regiment in Indochina, then in the 2nd Foreign Infantry Regiment, and finally he ended up with the Foreign Legion paratroopers. When one of us asked Johann the question: "What does it take to be a good boss?" he spontaneously replied: "A head. A heart, and balls in your pants!" Once more, an ancient – an antecessor – had shown us which way to take. His simple words, seasoned by experience, the missions and time, did in fact contain all the qualities a boss should have, if he wanted to lead his men to success. The emphasis is on 'lead', not meaning: ordering about! One is tempted to retort that this Johann Wallisch was a superior at a time that has been over for half a century, and that all of this is part of a military walk of life.

We must not be mistaken!

The ancient values are of more significance today than ever. They are the cornerstone of the greatest and most successful operations and responsible for the careers of the most famous tycoons in this world. And with regard to the military element, take that: It is not about the framework, it is all about the contents! To lead, to be boss and role model, all these are human adventures. A human adventure doesn't give a damn about the framework, it can be applied to any location, to any situation and to all areas, it may be transferred to any concept and to any sphere. I think I can be the judge of that, as my own way – not so dissimilar to Johann Wallisch's – showed me exactly that in an emphatic manner. My leadership positions – in particular those I held in the French Foreign Legion – and all the experience gained, have enabled me to skillfully implement 'successful leadership' in my civilian profession as a businessman to this very day. In the military in general, and in the Foreign Legion in particular, you basically learn two things: To obey, i.e. carry out orders, and to lead by example. The former is probably the most essential process for the latter. As the civilian Thomas Gast, I would collaborate with former legionnaires every now and then, in diverse positions and in the most outlandish locations on this planet. But I would also team up with men and women who had never been in the Legion, or in any other army for that matter. The difference was always striking. First, most ex-legionnaires would speak at least three languages, which facilitated our work no end. But that was not all. In the course of his affiliation with the Legion, the legionnaire will acquire virtues he benefits from in a civil workplace: Things like punctuality, reliability, loyalty, incorruptibility and know-how in all the fields pertaining to security. I have never heard a company boss complain about a former legionnaire, on the contrary. Especially in respect of security as well as in jobs that require organizational talent, there are a few reputable firms that take on ex-legionnaires by preference. Because of these virtues. Because of head, heart and balls!

One day, Wallisch, whom I met in my private life after my time in the Legion, said to me: "When I applied for the job of head supervisor import/export at Michelin Karlsruhe, there were two dozen other applicants. Amongst them numerous industrial engineers and business economists. I was the only one without a degree and without an excellent formal education. But I knew my way around people. And I was the only one to show up on time for the job interview. That's why I got the job." All of this speaks volumes: Knowledge of human nature and reliability! In brief, two of the many virtues that make a long-serving soldier. Wallisch got the job and he went on to erect his second successful pillar in the private sector.

For 'head', read intelligence.

For 'heart', read intuition or empathy.

For 'balls', read strength of character.

Intelligence: For somebody who must analyze a given, constantly changing situation; who must have a clear vision of what he wants; whose position demands to proactively and appropriately conceive an action, a plan or a policy (direction) – of whatever type –intelligence is indispensable for such a person. Without distinct (self-) cogitation, however, you will remain a staunch and disciplined executor or a wannabe-boss. You take the orders or instructions from higher echelons in your stride without understanding the logic behind them, not to mention looking for some sense, and you continue to pass down this horseshit.

Strength of character: The art of leadership, the art of being a boss, does not solely boil down to intelligence. It also hinges on the second pillar of strength of character. Here, it is all about the will to mobilize the women and men working for you. To have them unified behind you and to lead their soul, their combined power and their means to a common goal that needs to be attained: Success! We may have recourse to the saying: "Where there's a will, there's a way", or even "A hundred sheep, led by a lion, are more dangerous than a hundred lions, led by a sheep".

Empathy: The last, but not the least quality called for in leadership is intuition or empathy. We do not lead machines. We do not lead computers (yet). We lead human beings! These people are all our wealth, our own true treasure. It does not matter what you call the applied processes of the employer: Pedagogics, educational sciences, judgment, friendship, attention or simply heartfelt insight – if they are genuine, they will lead to mutual appreciation. Without it, the company is useless. In the absence of mutual respect – employer vs. employee – the enterprise is bound to fail in due course, rest assured of that. Head, heart and balls. All three at the same time and in equal proportion? Or head first, then heart and balls? Is there a sequence, a priority?

No.

Perhaps.

Absolutely.

Depending on which business building block or module we are at right now, the *a little more of the one*, and the *a little less of the other* can indeed be a bonus. A businessman – and when I say 'businessman', I mean everyone who assumes a leadership role – should handle the dose of more / less like a regimental commander. In peacetime, in training and maneuver (except in special cases such as concerning the safety of the staff), we have the subsequent order: Heart, head, balls. The boss might as well set aside his authority and strength of character, without losing them. What is needed here is the interhuman element. Mutual respect. Harmonious interactions as a forged community, because … "It is only with the heart that one can see rightly." (Antoine de Saint-Exupéry). When peacetime maneuvers are well planned – a plan is only ever good when it leaves scope for spontaneous alteration – well timed and when everything is well organized, then accidents, improvisation, haste and precipitance as well as unnecessary, evil adrenalin can almost be excluded. In return, the task must still be carried out in times of war: Sometimes at all cost. There will be casualties. People dying. Enemies. They have no heart but weapons. In such a situation, the boss must show strength, and force his will upon his men. So, strength of character is called for, first and foremost. A creative input by the executors is not exactly desirable here! Then comes the head (see intelligence). The intuition, or the empathy, only has restricted legitimization. To quote Clausewitz: "War is such a dangerous business that mistakes that come from kindness are the very worst." (Carl Philipp Gottfried von Clausewitz). In conclusion, I would like to point out that, should a boss fail to tie the employee to both himself and the company in peacetime (love: you are reading right), the selfsame person is going to leave him in the lurch in wartime. In return, love in war quickly mutates to what we call brotherhood in arms: The war is won! Now for the enterprise, the firm, the business. Let us replace the word 'war' by terms more likely used in the private sector: impending insolvency. Fight for competitiveness, pressure of competition. General inflation. Impending personnel cutbacks, sudden loss of distribution channels ... that's plenty.

Has the penny dropped?

THE BOSS's VADE MECUM OR THE 'TEN COMMANDMENTS'

I would like to take this opportunity to present you with a handout for the boss. I do indeed refer to them as 'the ten commandments'. It does not matter if you are a Siemens general manager or shelf supervisor at Lidl: Everyone who wants to be boss should take these commandments, these basic values, to heart.

First commandment: The boss is morally unimpeachable.

He seeks the truth, is honest and displays conduct that reflects openness and moral dignity. He is aware of his responsibility, and he does not shy away from it. He does not manipulate: Neither people nor results, numbers, figures, scales or charts. Unfair competition is anathema to him.

Second commandment: The boss is demanding.

Suffused by an intellectual discipline, he should be convinced – for his subordinates' sake as well as his own – that diligence in executing instructions is the first and best guarantor for success.

Third commandment: The boss is brave.

In everyday life, he represents his instructions, and he is fully accountable. If push comes to shove, he is at the forefront. He should be deeply convinced that, in order for his firm or company to meet with success, he will scale any barricade – be it high and in the crossfire of the competition and the public.

Fourth commandment: The boss is a man of convictions.

In principal, he is convinced that his superiors as well as his coworkers and subordinates will go to any length to ensure the smooth running of the shop. He conveys this positive attitude to all and sundry. He cultivates it permanently.

Fifth commandment: The boss is constantly on the alert.

The safety of his workforce is his main concern. Sound judgment and an even better assessment of potential hazards distinguish him. He might be risk-tolerant, but he will avoid the utterly superfluous ones.

Sixth commandment: The boss is human (e).

He permanently strives to be just and (as far as possible) impartial. He deliberately generates a climate of trust and cohesion. He will pay special attention to the weakest links. He gives everyone the same chance and shows consideration for personal, private and off-duty difficulties his employees may encounter. He caters to their needs. He makes time for them.

Seventh commandment: The boss is competent.

He could perform everything that he asks of his employees. Ideally, he masters all the necessary techniques his employees are constantly confronted with.

Eighth commandment: The boss is a role model.

By his demeanor (also cleanliness and choice of attire, the outfit). By his conduct (calm, assertive, modest). By his self-possession, but also by his hair wet with rain, dirty hands and feet in sludge!

Ninth commandment: The boss is loyal.

He is grateful. Grateful to be there. Grateful also to occupy this leadership role. And he exudes this gratitude.

Tenth commandment: The boss leads.

Always. In the rain. In a storm. In good times, but also when the proverbial shit hits the fan. He oozes success and he carries his employees along in this belief. He leads, but he does not order anyone about.

MARCH OR DIE – TOGETHER WE ARE STRONGER. REAL-LIFE EXAMPLE

The first scene unfolded during the Képi Blanc March (white headpiece of the legionnaires). This march led us across one hundred kilometers to the Pont du Gard. One stretch dragged on endlessly uphill. The rain bothered us, our shoulders sported the first sore spots, caused by the rucksack. We were hungry, our feet blistered and morale was fighting its first bitter battle. Suddenly my binôme – in the Legion, two men make one binôme – was by my side. He was limping and at the end of his tether. "Erdoğan is worn out", he sighed as he was marching stoically, head bent, alongside me. He did not want to fall behind since that would mean having to run uphill like hell. I slowed down a bit, looking around. Thompson, the Englishman, was trailing about ten meters behind in my tracks. He was carrying a second rucksack, which he had flung across his shoulders. By its nametag, I recognized the rucksack as belonging to Erdoğan.

"Where's the Turk?", I asked.

Thompson, who would not stop lest he lose his impetus, grinned when passing me by. "I've told the moron to piss in his boots before the march, so that the leather gets smooth. He wouldn't listen, typically Turk that he is. Stubborn dickheads, the lot of them!"

When we arrived on top of the mountain about fifteen minutes later, the platoon leader was standing at the wayside. He looked as neat as a pin, in spite of his own rucksack, heavier and larger than ours, on his back. His face was a mask, he had his hands folded on his chest, and he appeared to look towards us indifferently.

"Fall in!" His order was curt, concise and without withdrawal.

We quickly formed a row of three and took position of attention. We had some difficulty standing calm and upright.

The platoon leader came to a halt before Thompson. "Whose sack is this?" "That's soldier Erdoğan's sack, at your orders, mon adjudant-chef (sergeant-major)!"

"And where is soldier Erdoğan?"

His face was only half an inch from Thompson's.

"I don't know, mon adjudant-chef."

Romero, that was the platoon leader's name, wrinkled his nose.

"You do not know", he said stretching the words. "His binôme? Does soldier Erdoğan have something along the lines of a binôme?"

In the meantime, he had made it to the last row to come to stand exactly in front of Erdoğan's binôme who had thick sweat on his forehead, sweat that was not the least to do with exhaustion. He was ashen-faced.

"Don't you know either where your binôme is? And why are you not carrying his rucksack, but he?" He pointed at Thompson.

"I …"

"What are you?" – He was harshly interrupted by adjudant-chef Romero. He spit on the ground and showed him his clenched fist. "I'll show you what you are. A sordid canal rat what lets down its friend, that's what you are! If we were at the front, I would shoot you on the spot. All of you! And now, down with you, into the dirt. Rats belong in the dirt."

While we were busy crawling down the mountain on our bellies, commando-style, we heard his thundering voice, sounding ominously, above our heads.

"Legionnaires stick together. Nobody is left behind, ever, you hear me? NEVER! It's not enough to learn the legionnaires' code of honor by heart, you must live it. Liiiiive!"

We continued belly-crawling downhill until there were holes in our trousers, and the sighs of some were louder than the voice of the adjudant-chef. Erdoğan had come to lie at the bottom of the mountain, his ankles swollen. The platoon was complete, again. Our superior's actions had enormous effects on us all. We were ashamed, as we had nearly missed the most essential element, or, to be more explicit: We had experienced something of essential significance. Something, upon which the strength of the Foreign Legion hinged. The team spirit, esprit de corps, cohesion. In retrospect, I can say that nothing of that kind ever happened to us again. Adjudant-chef Romero had of course been noticing that one man continued to fall behind. He could have made us halt. Granted a respite. This, however, he deliberately did not do. He had us march on instead. It was a test. We had acted like a maverick, but at the height of the battle, not been able to act as a team. The sense of unity – WE – was simply not there. Oh surely we would have won the next battle, but lost the war. Now delete 'Foreign Legion', insert Daimler, Aldi, Allianz or BMW. Do you notice something? When calling upon our cohesion, Romero also called upon the company philosophy and upon the (your?) long-standing corporate culture. Only together we are strong!

PRESERVING THE EMPLOYEES' INTEGRITY. REAL-LIFE EXAMPLE

Well then! The following scene also evolved in Haiti. At the very beginning of my duties as Country Manager there was a local meeting of one of my financial bosses – let's call him Brandon –, the incumbent EU security officer, and myself. Brandon was in charge of the economic section, whereas I was in charge of the technical / operational one. Both obviously had some problems with the local employees, or at least they were not pleased with the guys on patrol. At the meeting Brandon, who was always thinking US-dollars, suggested buying bugs and listening devices for the clandestine wiretapping of the employees' conversation. I was meant to install these 'gadgets' in the patrol cars and different workplaces. In addition, he wanted to pay informers who should constantly report back to him on the contents of these conversations. He reckoned that for 50 US-dollars, each of the 'local guards' would sell his own grandmother. As the EU security officer (also my superior) had no objection and seemed rather happy with this option, I kept quiet. Of course I realized at once that the gentlemen simply wanted to check on their own watchmen without compunction. Not the mission, but their surveillance was their priority. They wanted to know when, where and how long the guards would take a break. And they wanted to hear rebellious and compromising conversations, by all means. I thought they hadn't thought it through, and I set score by a little more trust. What if the guards were to take an extra break or two during their eight-hour shift, what of it? That was fine. That was only fair. And gossiping is part of the job, who was I to reinvent the wheel? As long as they did not overdo it. After the meet with the security officer and Brandon, I went over the talk word by word in my head. Personally, I arrived at the following conclusion: As long as I had some saying in the matter, I would permit no one to take advantage of the Haitians. Bugs and listening devices were illicit in Europe, why should it be any different here, in Haiti? Paying informers? That was totally out of the question. With London (headquarters of the general manager) and Brandon in CC, I wrote to the security officer on that very same evening. It was a polite, but firm mail. I informed him about what I thought of the issue that we had discussed, and that I was strictly against it.

What had I done?

- **I had taken an unambiguous stand against my superiors, and in favor of my employees.**
- **I was fair (there were not a few who said I had been foolish in the highest degree).**
- **I had put my job on the line.**

- **I had preserved the integrity of 135 employees.**
- **I had stuck my neck out and sent a signal for the future and for my employees.**

In spite of the heavy flak I was getting, I felt great. Only that this is another example that whispered to me: Leadership, that means to constantly have your hands in the dirt, up to your elbows!

A SIMPLE QUESTION

One of the questions most often put to me was: How do you lead in the Foreign Legion?

My spontaneous reply was: With heavy pads to joint success! To leave it like that does not make a lot of sense, naturally, although the core messages are already there:

The road is rocky and long.

Nothing is left to chance.

In the end joint success is the reward.

Is this confusing? Good! So let me rephrase the question.

What makes a leader?

First, there is a cast-iron principle: Only he who has learned to lead himself can lead successfully. A little further down in the text you will find words like authority and discipline. Rest assured: You cannot do without them. Now I am going to give you another word without which it will not work either, although you might erroneously think it utterly misplaced. The word love.

Love your staff!

If you, as a leader, do not manage to picture yourself, your company in general, your department, your section and your personnel in particular, as one big family, then you are out of place. Then you have no right to occupy the boss's chair. My advice: Identify wholly and unreservedly with your company (your family) and make sure you do get this across.

... you do love your family, after all?

As a leader, you are a man of the heart. All of your staff's concerns are your concerns as well, so take care of them. Good times, bad times: Share both with them, since there is one irrefutable certainty – you are all in the same boat. Authority, discipline and a cool distance are the framework, and this trinity does not contradict the aforesaid. But beware. No matter what happens, remember: You are you! No other human being on this planet is like yourself. Do not try to be somebody else or to emulate someone you worship. Remain true to yourself. Come across as being authentic! Always stay yourself and acquire leadership characteristics in due course that shape you and your personal character, that make you even more unique. Good leadership is based upon three pillars.

THREE PILLARS – 1. RESPECT

The success story. One of my masterpieces in terms of leadership happened rather late in my life, in August 2008, to be precise. At the time, I did not know whether it would turn out "well" or whether I was headed towards disaster. To cut a long story short, it was excellent! With hindsight, this action represents everything I had learned throughout my long years as a leader. An action which expresses to me the following: Power, determination and courage of a genuine leader, a true superior, but also his capability to give to the people what is the people's, to see the needs of the subordinates and to create a common basis – we are all pulling together!

Place of action: Haiti. This was the situation. Before I started in my new job, the London bosses told me upfront that this would not be an easy task, and that I would encounter nothing but problems. Before I boarded my flight, I already knew that Haiti was one of the poorest countries in the world and that Haiti's children, the women and men of this island (i.e. also our local personnel there) were said to be the proudest denizens of this world. For good measure, they were rather ill advised with the governing body we had in place there. In other words, there were issues regarding the (French) management of roughly 145 indigenous employees. My predecessor, a former colonel in the regular French army, told me a lot. He was on about an insubordinate, uncooperative, unable and lazy bunch. He talked of languid employees and their constant and inacceptable demands for pay rise, financial adaption of cost of living and so on, and on! And he told me about their hatred of us Europeans and about visceral rejection. When I finally arrived in Haiti to begin my new job (I was meant to relieve him as boss), I was most surprised to find out that the lazy bunch was not the 145 indigenous employees, but the four European team leaders who were supposed to support me in my work. With every day passing, I noticed that, concerning leadership, these well-qualified professionals did nearly everything wrong that could be done wrong. At once, I entered into intensive employee dialogues. At first with my team leaders, and then with all the 'natives'. I had a serious word with them, one after another. Within three days of my working incessant sixteen-hour days, I managed to get the picture. Basically, there could be no doubt about the fact that the hundred or so women and men, whose professionalism and skills, reliability and loyalty in respect of the British firm we were all working for on behalf of the European Commission, constituted a great asset. Exactly that sort of asset which – in order to evoke greatest client satisfaction

– I urgently needed, and on which I wouldn't have to waste any thought under ordinary circumstances. An asset, however, that now lay barren because it could not be put to optimal use. The evaluation of my talks resulted in me listing the subsequent mistakes regarding the virtual non-functioning or failure of the firm at that point.

- **Haughtiness on the part of the European team leaders and my predecessor.**

- **Intolerance.**

- **Massive misjudgment of human resources.**

- **Arrogance.**

In simple terms: Incompetence of the superiors incumbent.

I did have some concept – if only vague – but I was also a little bit baffled. What should I do to get the machinery of success going again? Where to start in order to get back on track, back on the road to success?

The final talk definitely confirmed my thoughts that had at best been vague up to that point. It was a talk with somebody from the lower ranks, with a person who – at least if seen from above – was one of the last links in the chain. I am talking about the villa gardener. He was an old, amiable man with greying temples. At the time, he earned about forty dollars per month, but his advice was worth more than gold. In the course of the polite dialogue, which I conducted in a slightly aloof way, as was my wont, he pointed at the flagpole in front of the villa. The Tricolour (French flag – 'le tricolore') was happily flying in the wind.

"We are the first black state to have gained independence!"

Upon which a veil descended upon his face, and he just turned away from me.

I had gotten the message!

At once did I ask my chief secretary to get hold of a Haitian flag, the largest he could find, and to erect a second pole right next to the one already in place. At the same time, I issued my first circular mail, my first directive. Without exception, all employees of the firm were to gather for my inaugural address that was scheduled for the next morning, on the lawn in front of the villa. There, before 145 employees, the team leaders and a few invited guests, I concisely laid down my company philosophy and my leadership style that was mainly based upon three pillars, as we shall see further on.

At the end of the speech, my secretary hoisted the flag of Haiti to the mast that had been erected overnight. The response was not long in waiting. The act was accompanied by roaring applause, an applause that would last for minutes, an applause that was liberating: Energies were set free, desires were set free ... joy of working was released!

An insubordinate, uncooperative, unable and lazy bunch of sluggish employees had, at the drop of a hat, become a guild of employees, ready to devote itself unreservedly to the firm, and to gladly do overtime with a smile. All of a sudden, the motivation of the employees was back, and the prestige of the firm grew, as did customer satisfaction. In a flash, the firm was back to the place it deserved.

Number one! The firm!

How was all that possible?

Well, the first pillar to buttress the bridge that leads where we all want to be, had come into play.

Its name?

Respect.

I acted respectfully in the highest degree.

Respect.

If you don't have it, everything will blow up in your face sooner or later.

Respect

Always passes over into trust, and without having the trust of your employees, or, the other way round, without putting trust in your employees, you are nothing, since respect and the resulting trust are stones that make a rock. They are amongst the essential keys to success. But beware. At the risk of repeating myself, it is not all about one and the same direction. I am talking about the respect you owe to your subordinates – see the aforementioned example – but also about the respect that is owed to you. Let's continue with the latter.

… the respect that is owed to you.

In order to get that, the leaders need competency, irrespective of their level. Human, i.e. social and professional competence. An employee who has just started in his new posting, and who sees you for the first time, will not be able to judge either of those. He did not have the time. What he can and will judge, however, is your initial demeanor vis-à-vis him. This demeanor will stick to him, is glued to him, and it puts you into the drawer that bears your name.

The mission brought me nothing but trouble. By hoisting the Haitian flag, I had set the ball rolling that triggered a whole landslide. Barely ten minutes after this highly symbolic action, the phones were ringing off the hook at all critical spots in town. Within but a few minutes I had taken on the entire French Community, all the French living in Haiti. Men and women who had never seen me before would whisper when they saw me. Not because they wanted to pin a medal on my chest. Yet, to me this was part and parcel of being a boss: To preserve my employees' interests! To expose myself to inconvenience! To not always do what is popular at the moment! To be human (e) even if too much tolerance could cost me my job! Not to kiss up, kick down, just because a bonus, some winnings or royalties are tempting, or just because a promotion might be due!

THREE PILLARS – 2. AUTHORITY

The success story: In 1987, I was still a rather young soldier, when I was transferred from French-Guiana to the Legion's paratroopers in Corsica (with eulogies, regarding the receiving regiment, in my ears, top of the heap, élite, cream of the crop, best of the best), and what I first saw was my future leader. This is still the prevailing impression I have when thinking back.

Why?

I am going to tell you in a nutshell! You will understand.

I am talking about the following situations: You start afresh in the firm, you have leadership tasks and it is your first day, your first meeting with the employees. Or you have just been promoted, suddenly find yourself in a superior position, etc.

In front of me – cool and keeping a distance – there stood a man of medium height, with his hair cropped short, his chin chiseled, and a piercing stare. He wanted us to put stones in our rucksacks that were too heavy already. Then, we should slave away, running across 9.5 kilometers. The superior himself? Absolutely confident demeanor. Taciturn. Never said anything twice. Took decisions instantly when they were called for. Punishments would follow on the spot. In the beginning, he lumped all of us together (at least he did so up until the moment when the wheat was separated from the chaff, and when he delegated certain tasks to those he deemed able). Summary: There never was and there never will be (once certain requirements are met) a doubt about who was, or who will be, calling the shots. Before us, there stood no skeptic.

Now … to the posse of rookies in front of him, amongst them me, it never occurred for one second not to do exactly as the instructor told them. Had he ordered us to jump off the roof of a three-story building, it would have happened. We were enthralled by his authority. Instinctively – and that seems to be the crux – we sensed that the man before us would only ask of us what he himself could do (to prove: the rucksack by his side seemed bigger than ours) and that everything that he ordered was only to our own benefit. To our own benefit, which automatically was in the best interest of all, and the best for the company. So far so good, but now for the unrelenting truth. Everyone listening to the words and instructions of the alpha leader in front of us, at once had the same thought, the significance of which is enormous …

   … of enormous importance to you!

This thought was that all of us would unconditionally follow the instructions of the boss, and not mainly for the reason that he was the superior, but because a vision was beginning to form in our heads, which read: Some day, I want to be exactly like him!

This demeanor, the entire posture, impressed me and at once conveyed to me a sense of security. "The man in front of me is not some joker, he is my boss." Later, when I was a boss, I had adopted a similar, if personalized posture – because it worked.

Authority.

With success!

Conclusion: The demeanor of a boss must never come across as hesitant, half-hearted or frightened. Self-confident. "We are who we are – and I am I", as a certain Van Gaal, then coach of FC Bayern Munich, once put it (at a time when he had no idea how the forthcoming season would end). The first impression, and what it meant to me then?

… piercing stare:

He misses nothing.

… self-confident demeanor:

He knows the goal.

… taciturn:

No bullshitter.

… never said anything twice:

Means just what he says.

… punishments would follow on the spot:
Beware!

… took decisions instantly when they were called for:

He has no backlog. The man is goal- and victory-oriented.

… at first lumped us all together:

Treats everyone the same way. Acts justly. Whilst consciously taking in the skills and character of all and sundry in order to use them in such a way that later on everyone could thrive according to their skills and character. 'Just' only works to the end of the road. That is often when winding paths commence, those of individual self-fulfillment.

… has a rucksack too, that guy:

Cries the same tears as us.

If a superior manages to get all of these features across at his introduction, when making his debut, his first appearance as a leader, he has already won half of his employees over. Although the competency question – at least the professional one – has not in the least been clarified yet. And the other half? Will follow suit as soon as all competency questions (professional and social) have definitely been resolved. You can tell from experience that somebody who makes such a self-confident appearance will not be a professional non-entity. Not all of us have the privilege of looking like Daniel Craig or George Clooney, with piercing stare and steel-grey eyes and blessed with a body like Charles Bronson. And it is not about that, either. It is about your personal self-confident demeanor, period. Authority (just like all the other pillars of my leadership concept) is something you can learn. It is very rarely that you are born with it.

Someday I want to be exactly like him!

At the start of your career – no matter if it is the Legion or a million other comparable job situations – there can be no cooperative leadership style. What we need, by all means, is authority. Be authoritative (authoritative with a C like competence and not with an L as in loudmouth!) Keep a cool distance. This very authority is the second pillar upon which your success will rest.

THREE PILLARS – 3. DISCIPLINE

The success story: Quite possibly the most crucial pillar. Always demonstrate the highest level of discipline, and demand this from your employees. Discipline has many features – too many to give names to all of them. The following story, also included in 'Leben unter fremder Flagge' (*Life under a Foreign Flag*; my autobiographical reminiscences, published in 2016) sounds trivial. At first glance, it might take place at the highest levels, but I can reassure you, my dear reader: Each and every tiny link in the hierarchy had contributed its share so that the simple story became a story of success.

In May 1997, our regiment in Kinshasa / Congo was to conduct a large-scale combat mission. It was about the liberation of civilians from a town that looked as if it would become the scene of a bloody war. We were still in high-speed preparation in Brazzaville, when a phenomenon began to loom, something we had rarely encountered. On all levels, the reins slackened a little, never mind the discipline … war would only start the following day, and that was still a long time. OK, in this case we did not really know when the mission would be given the green light.

Fancy a bit of the old party mood before the thunderstorm?

Sure! The men frequented the bars at night and got drunk. And African women – all sorts of imaginable diseases in the crotch – were swirling around them like bees around a honeypot.

Having condoned the activities for a while, our regimental commander suddenly saw the mission jeopardized. He had every right to worry, and so he did the only right thing. He called upon us leaders, called upon the discipline of each and every one of our men, and he gave an inflammatory speech that is still echoing in my ears. He said:

"When Paris decides that we go to war, we are the damned best soldiers in the world. And when they (those in Paris) decide that we must clean all the shithouses of Paris … then we are the damned best shithouse-cleaners of the world, and afterwards, there won't be a city on this planet, whose shithouses are cleaner."

It was a reminder that discipline plays a role even when the mission is still far away. It was a call for contemplating that as leaders, we have to assume responsibility right now. Demand discipline and live discipline. From then on, we would do just that, and precisely that was wanted. An immediate curfew was imposed. We drilled the legionnaires to exhaustion, bravely suffered alongside them. Notices were given, and we offered what our men took in their stride without complaining: The party was over! The mission was not long in waiting, and success was resounding, something that was reflected in the hymns of praise in the international press.

Success through discipline.

Translated into the private sector, no matter what area, discipline also and above all means the following:

Punctuality.

As a leader, you are well advised to be there, and ready for action, rather earlier than last-minute, and never be the first to leave your workplace at the stroke of the gong. In return, expect punctuality from your employees.

Appearance.

Set store by your (neat) appearance. I do not mean personal hygiene, as I assume you've got this one right, otherwise you wouldn't be where you are. I mean … how do others see me, my boss, the client, my employees? Why don't you look in the mirror and scrutinize yourself before leaving your home (on time) in the morning? The look must play along! Affirmative … we are all very tolerant and nobody is going to hold it against you when, off-duty, you get your I-am-a-rocker-leather-jacket out of the closet, and leap onto a motorcycle to shoot off to your regular haunt, draped in flesh tunnels, piercings and earrings. But, as I have said: after office hours!

Discipline is also about modesty and sacrifice, so be humble, practice self-denial and get your employees in the same boat with you. Demand discipline, live discipline!

GAME OVER – LEADERSHIP AND SURVIVAL

There is no better learning field than survival to mentally prepare executives, top managers and team leaders for what 'hardcore' awaits them in the corporations and enterprises. No means is more effective than regular outdoor activities, if you want to render seasoned executives even more efficient, more stress-resistant and resilient. The best French officer candidates at the reputed French Military Academy of Saint-Cyr (in fact managers-to-be, in charge of 120 to 1,200, and more, employees) are sent to French Guiana to take part in a survival course in the Legion's jungle camp. Once they pass, they are fit for all "higher" tasks that their career has in store. The system is time-proven. What about German companies sending their executives on a three- to five-day survival course once a year – instead of having them attend the annual staff outing in a top hotel with jolly workshops, lush buffets, boring sightseeing tours and all the other luxury you can imagine? If I were general manager, I would take an interest in whether my executives, ... many of which are used to sitting in squeaky clean and air-conditioned offices, where they administer people, commodities or their production via computer-based programs, and comfortably give their instructions over the phone, from an armchair ... would still retain their composure and skills, when they are:

- **Tired, hungry and irritable**

- **Soaked to the bones by the rain, freezing**

- **Filthy and sweaty ...**

... would have to lead a group in the field and in an "assumed" survival situation (lead, and not slave-drive them).

Would my top-earners still prevail as manager when asked, ... out there, outdoors ... even in the worst assumable situation, to keep on giving coherent, clear and above all, convincing instructions? What if, under described circumstances, they were to demonstrate how to slaughter an animal to drink its blood, how to set up a trap or to orientate cross-country in difficult terrain, armed only with map and compass, all the while being scrutinized (by a squad of six men in their wake)? Would they still be able to prove their intelligence and efficiency (for which I have hired them)?

But this is not all; it is about so much more. Short courses of this type are conducive to all leadership qualities, thereby rendering the company more competitive/viable at all levels. In particular, the development extends to:

Team spirit or ésprit de corps

It encourages the identification with the company and the WE-feeling, and ultimately solidarity and loyalty!

Stress resistance

The advantages of a boss, who is stress-resistant, are obvious. The first thing to benefit is the capacity to perform.

Poise

A balanced boss really is something. One cannot help but imitate his attitude. The effect? An overall better satisfaction at work!

Self-confidence / respect

Self-confidence positively represents the firm to the exterior. A boss will automatically be shown respect if he exudes aplomb and pays respect to the employees and colleagues. Whether outside in the hot and humid mangrove forest or within the cool company walls: Nothing will work without respect!

Self-discipline and discipline in general

Makes everything more profitable. Discipline promotes rationality; hence, it is the "saving factor". At least it does not deplete the coffers.

Successful outdoor activities foster the "clout" of the boss, his "ingenuity and creativeness" as well as his "keen assessment", the "fast weighing of the odds" within seconds, but also the "in-depth reflection". These are all attributes a modern executive should have at their disposal. The hands-on experience of survival gives you an appetite for starting each day anew, full of energy, because you have succeeded and are now inspired by a winner's mentality; and because you know: "Game over" is another time!

PRIVATE MATTERS ON DUTY

Do not waste the time you are getting paid for on personal matters. Nobody is angry with you, should you call your own home when the wife or children are ill, when you urgently have to send an important private e-mail or cast a furtive glance in some newspaper or other, every once in a while! But do not overdo it. Be a role model; leave your (party-, banter- and gossip-) cellphone on mute (silent mode). Restrict personal calls to the breaks, and read your papers at home in the evening, it is cozier there anyway. As you display discipline, you have every right to rant if your employees should not observe all of this. I will not continue for I believe you have already caught my drift.

MARGINAL REFLECTIONS

The getting to know each other *boss – employees* need not be enforced by 'close proximity'. Especially not when you are not a 'close' boss as, for example, the department head, the squad leader, the leader of a small team, the foreman or the 'overseer'. What we are talking about here, is the handshake. It does not always make sense to shake hands with the employees / the subordinates at the very first meeting. Here, less is often more. A handshake – even if it is meant to express warmth and attachment – takes the edge away from that cool distance that you, as a much higher-ranking superior, should have at any rate. You may shake hands as much and as often as you want to (a very German thing, by the way), but not straight away, and not at every occasion. Reserve the handshake for exceptional situations. For instance, when conducting an inspection or visit. If, on that special occasion, you also call the employee by his or her name, you score. This is important. But still ...

Less is often more!

The statement stands. Simply think in practical terms: When you are far away, you can still come near enough to touch the bacon. If you have come too close already, the jackals will eat your entrails.

You are the boss!

No doubt about that.

One might retort that a genuine boss may shake hands till he's black in the face, without having to suffer a loss of prestige. I wholly agree with that. But let's be honest: True leaders are not a dime a dozen, and these leaders would perhaps not have to buy this book. A sympathetic smile, however, is always appropriate, no matter if it's boom times or general depression is in the air, and we all know: A smile is the shortest distance between two people! You should also staunchly refrain from calling your junior employees by their first name. Mutual respect cuts both ways – it is of the essence. In the end, your integrity might hinge upon those trifles.

✓ **Not "Peter is a rock", but YOU ARE A ROCK!**

Did I say conference?

Meeting?

There are certain situations when you have to communicate with the employees on a regular basis. Or you should. First and foremost, in the beginning, during the stages of onboarding or when problems crop up. Many parameters will determine who attends a meeting or a conference; but for goodness' sake, do not get into the habit of wanting to explain the minutest ins-and-outs to everybody, all the time. To pass on information is good, to roust and upset the people, however, is counterproductive. It would often be better to form a small team of experts, which is working intensely and meticulously to resolve a problem, and which is exclusively informed about such an issue.

N.B.: On a mission, it was important to me that all my legionnaires knew in detail what was going on. The soldier needs to be informed! This has always been my point of view. On a mission in conflict or war zones it is all about life or death. A lack of data knows no mercy. It was always easier for my legionnaires to go to war for some cause, once they knew in detail beforehand what was going on.

To which I counterpose the behavior of the Legion's bosses when, in January 2013, my unit set about parachuting into Timbuktu (Mali) under combat conditions in order to attack the town, which had been occupied by Islamist rebels. In Calvi (our garrison in Corsica) our regiment had been put on alert, and it was ready to go within few hours. In general, total discretion was the order of the day. The legionnaires (staff officers exempt) did not know what to expect, where the place of deployment was and when it would start against whom. And if they were to "think aloud", they were condemned to keep quiet. On January 23, this African Detachment was committed to Abidjan, the capital of the Ivory Coast. The Legion's paras were still unaware of the fact that a bespoke guerilla mission was in the offing for them. The impending mission was bathed in strict secrecy. Nobody knew the operational area, no one was allowed to make phone calls. They even collected the cellphones: total radio silence. Silence Radio (as we say in French). In brief: The men were not getting even the tiniest snippet of information!

It is a similar situation with most civilian jobs – sometimes, the employees must be informed of everything, and then again – under different framework conditions – it is better if they know nothing.

The issue of the handshake can be clarified during the first talk with the employee. And also, the one with the first names. If you need to make decisions, so make them, that is why you are a leader, but beware of permanently justifying your decisions in front of your subordinates. This will, more often than not, backfire. You do not ask either, whether the subordinate condones your decision (N.B.: Sometimes this needs to be done!) since s/he might say 'no' in spite of your conviction that yours is the right decision. What then?

Do not ask – decide!

Very important: Never ask of your employees anything you could not do yourself. Ideally, you have already occupied the employee's chair, and you used to perform just as well or even better than her/him today. You could act as a role model any time, you know the job. If there is a corporate personnel office dealing with such issues as vacation, salaries, remuneration, accounting, etc., then try not to get involved. Above all, do not make promises you cannot keep. This question needs to be addressed and resolved: As a leader, where are the limits of my competencies regarding the domain of HR, admin, etc.?

LOOKING THE OTHER WAY?

A little anecdote on the side, so you see that there are, or should be, situations in which you have to slacken the reins and look the other way. In 1991, we had a Rallye Group in Chad – I had been a squad leader for a year (in charge of 10 men). What that was all about is easily explained. There were thirteen or fourteen squads in our company. With the aim of fostering a healthy rivalry, and in order to constantly enhance the training, our company commander decided to organize this group 'rallye' where about ten different stations had to be passed. Within a time-limit, of course. It started with an 8,000 meter-run in full gear, followed by diverse technical stops, such as putting on the parachutes against time, disassembling our weapons blindfolded, shooting under difficult physical conditions and so on and on and on.

It is common practice in the regiment that only a victory counts or at best an outstanding performance. If you end up in second place or if the performance is 'merely' good, nobody will pay much attention, since a good performance is standard where we come from. At the end of the rallye, my squad came in second; we had missed the goal of being at the top of the podium by one or two points, and by a few seconds. My men were tired after being on watch duty for a whole week in some desert fort; they had endured long patrols at night and had not had any preparation time for that rallye, either. Still, they enjoyed the competition tremendously.

So be it!

The morning after the rallye, I had the squad line up at 06:00 hours for PT (physical training/sports). In silence, their faces slightly grim, they would run behind me for nearly ten kilometers until the trail disappeared into a valley path. They were quite amazed: On an even surface on the valley path, among some trees, there was our squad vehicle. Two tables had been laid with white paper cloth, on which there were two bottles of ice-cold champagne, chilled beer and other beverages as well as sandwiches and croissants. None of my men had expected this. I had clandestinely organized everything, even the platoon leader did not learn about it until the last second. I did not tell the men that I was proud of their (of our) performance, oh no! I did not mention yesterday's rallye with a single word, and yet: They could read the pride in my eyes. We drank to the health of our squad and to the health of our family (the enterprise). We had some excellent discussions, there was laughter and a bit of a sing-song, and two hours later we returned to camp by truck, and I gave the rest of the forenoon off: Quartier libre for all!

While on duty: Champagne and time-out ordered by the boss! Believe me – it has the impact of a 250-pound grenade!

Naturally, I had squared all of this with my superior – bar the wine and champagne. This gesture yielded me a little more of what a leader thoroughly enjoys: prestige! What makes these small gestures even more successful is the fact that nobody expects them, but everybody is still talking about them favorably, months after. Finally, and this is a crucial realization, I had noted – me included – that this Group Rallye had been huge fun for us. My conclusion here is: Only if you really enjoy your work, you can achieve something really good.

SUMMARY OF PART 1 OF THE BOOK

The three pillars, upon which a good leadership style rests, are:

- ✓ *Respect*

- ✓ *Authority*

- ✓ *Discipline*

Always remain authoritarian and distanced, yet do retain this (and point to it, occasionally): Each of your employees is a treasure trove! Everything is possible! Everyone has their place! Everybody is important!

Never ask anything of your employees you could not do yourself: Leading by example! You have made the most significant step as a leader once your employees follow your instructions and say to themselves – brilliant: I want to be like him! (… and not thinking: This is my boss, I had better do what he says!). Love your employees! Hoist a flag for them! Demand discipline and be a living example of discipline! Surprise your team / department every now and then (particularly, when they least expect it) and bear in mind: A smile is the shortest distance between two people! You are a rock!

LECTURE HALL AND FRONTLINE – IT'S GETTING SERIOUS!

In 1995, I spent a couple of weeks in beautiful Montpellier in the South of France. Then and there, at the École d'Application de l'Infanterie / the Infantry School, my most important and probably most career-advancing course was about to commence at national level. Should I pass this course, it would mean almost instantaneous promotion to the next rank as well as responsibility for forty-five men. When putting this so nonchalantly – responsibility for forty-five men – I mean, and I am being serious, the whole package: In this particular case, responsibility meant being an arbiter of life. The young people we are entrusted with do not come to work in the morning and go home at night – no! To them, BEING a LEGIONNAIRE equals life (or death), and all aspects of life – joy, suffering, emotion, hatred, daily planning, schedules, leisure, education, health, success or failure, good morning and good night ... all of that was now in my hands (if feelings and emotions can ever entirely be in somebody's hands other than your own). Well: The final core task of the course I had to master was the following: Every participant was given the supervision of a group of about 14 extras who were to do or act out exactly as they were told, no more, no less. The aim was to generate an exposé with their help, which the participant in charge had to present as his own to high-ranking officers; this would be followed by grading, etc. The time to draw up the exposé was short. After announcing the subject to my group, I at first went over to the other rooms to find out how the other participants would tackle their task. Just like me, they had distributed some sheets, announced the topic and the extras were already busy writing, each to themselves, they were diligently working in silence. In another hall there was fierce discussion amidst sheer pandemonium, and someplace else the participant had sent his extras on a cigarette break as, according to himself, he did not know what to do with these morons. At once I felt something rebelling inside of me and I instinctively did something daring. I asked the extras where they came from, what their educational background and their aptitudes were. Next, I formed three groups that would best fit my group analysis, I appointed one person each as boss and spokesman, and I gave them a subtopic for the exposé subject as well as a timeframe. Each of the three groups was to collectively get out the best in them to present their result in front of the whole group. If it was good, then we would continue to piece the best elements together in one single exposé: in my exposé!

To get the best out of each individual within a collective frame!

It was with alacrity that they set about their new task, and lo and behold: I ended up with the best thesis of all.

Who has brought me success?

Correct.

Highly motivated employees!

HOW DO YOU EXPERIENCE THE SUBJECT OF LEADERSHIP IN A SITUATION OF CRISIS?

And now: Let's get out of the lecture hall and onto the frontline. 1993 was a year that taught us an exemplary lesson in terms of leadership.

Who was it that taught us?

Well, our employees!

We were scheduled for a humanitarian mission during the Bosnian War. From the very beginning, this felt to us like the word 'nightmare'. I would like to elaborate on that. Our unit – from the smallest employee up to the CO (commanding officer) – had the reputation of an attack force. To wage war was our profession, and a theater of war was like a fish tank in which we could splash about like in our home waters, feeling comfortable. There was no unknown in this world of warriors. Suddenly, however, we were expected not to wage war, but to prevent a war and, it being in full swing already, to limit the damage. In other words: If we were under fire, we would not be allowed to respond with our extremely tough arguments. Should we encounter suffering and misery, we would have to stay neutral, and if we had an opinion, this was not always desirable. One of our tasks consisted of preventing heavily armed Bosnian fighters from their attempts at crossing Sarajevo Airport at nighttime.

No problem! Our world! This we could do!

We were really into it. Sleeves up, and if nice words didn't do the trick, as was to be expected, we would, at short notice, turn into something the world already knew us to be: Elite soldiers who had to carry out a task!

But … among those who tried to cross the airfield, besides the fighters, there were women with their babies, children, old people, the wounded, startled and sick war-torn souls, and so on and on and on. And there were artists and teachers.

And the poor and the rich: One people!

All they wanted was – to survive.

Consciously or subconsciously, they all acted upon the innermost wish and instinct of ALL human beings.

To be free!

And we?

Were in their way, as simple as that. You can well imagine that there were tears. Begging, pleading, invocations, shouts of abuse, a drama unfolding before our eyes (in this sector, people died and were

injured every hour in those nights steeped in history).
Soon I realized that our crack soldiers had a heart.
They no longer followed our orders and instructions
blindly, but they were trying to help, to mediate and
to facilitate. One of them, a Spaniard – a fighter and
genuine soldier in my platoon, refused to comply. He
could no longer watch that misery and pretend it was
nothing to do with him. As I was his direct superior, I
had to summon him before he would be turned over
to his platoon leader. I knew that, through his
behavior, he was heading for a fall, that it could cost
him his career, since a professional soldier who, for
whatever reasons, refuses to serve, is bound to
receive a respective entry in his personnel records,
and would have little or no chance at all to advance in
his job. While a war was raging outside, I sat in my
dugout, pondering. I had three options to bring the
stubborn guy to his senses or to deal with the case
before sending him to the lieutenant who would
definitely have no time for deep questions. He would
butcher the soldier on paper. Period!

Option number one.

The hard way! For men only – extremely painful. He
was used to that, it might have had some effect. I had
my doubts.

Option number two.

The ignorant administrative way! Which consisted of letting him walk straight into the trap, to his downfall. Apparently, he didn't want it any other way. I didn't like it.

Option number three.

My way! Which could break my neck … or it could help me become a rock.

Option number three was right up my street. With it, I felt most comfortable. I reflected upon what was happening out there in dark nights, and at daytime, before our very eyes. The question I then asked myself was the following. If it cannot be helped that one expects us (the commander from his officers, the officer from his non-commissioned officers, and the NCOs from their soldiers) to switch from elite soldier to philanthropist overnight (the one never excludes the other: to the contrary!), then I, on behalf of all the leaders in our unit, should be capable of finding and operating the switch that would open up other venues than the normal internal practice of having recourse to disciplinary measures. What I wanted was not a strict application of existing processes. The soldier was one of my men – and had he served in a different era, he would have faced a firing squad for insubordination. I needed him. He was unable to cope with a clearly defined psychological situation. Instead of punishing him, he needed help, and he needed it in such a way that it would neither impede him or his leaders, ever.

When the soldier appeared in my shelter, his face was taut. I thought he looked like somebody on his way to the gallows, somebody who still held to his view that he had done everything right, all the time.

"What do you want?" I asked.

"Away from here."

"How is your wife, your children?"

The soldier was taken aback, he had expected anything but this question. His tense facial expression began to relax. Warmth was creeping into his slightly reddened cheeks. It seemed as if he had seen me for the first time, that day.

"I ... I don't know. It's been ages since I had any news from home."

At the time, we only had two satellite telephones for roughly 400 men at our disposal. In addition, the tariff was exorbitant. They asked for fifty francs a minute, (about €8 in today's money). I laughed.

"Has your youngest one not been skiing recently?"

Total incomprehension was engulfing his face.

"Well", I continued. "And he wasn't careful, so he hurt his leg. It's a nasty, complicated and tricky fracture, isn't it? I think you should see for yourself if everything's all right at home!"

"Jesus, sergeant!"

That was all he could say before I allowed him to leave.

A few moments later I was sitting in the lieutenant's office. I cannot recall the exact words I had dug up from the chasms of my personal dictionary, but in the end, the lieutenant was totally convinced. The next day our soldier found himself on board a Russian Antonov, heading towards Zagreb. One day later he was at home with his family. That his son had never been skiing in all his life, remained our secret. It was no secret to me, however, that from then on, this soldier would always serve loyally and reliably, and he would volunteer for everything.

For EVERYTHING!

Conclusion?

Be authoritarian. Keep a cool distance, do not shake hands unless it cannot be avoided, and do not necessarily call the employees you respect by their first name. Be a rock … but do occasionally jump in at the very deep end for your employees! Risk everything for new visions by chucking out the old stuff! You would be surprised to see how open and receptive your bosses can be.

Will you proverbially dive head first into very cold waters for your staff?

And by 'cold' I mean minus 120 degrees and not manageably lukewarm.

It is in these moments of great decisions, at the crossroads, innovations that you must keep a close eye on your employees. When you notice that they are tense, unable to cope, looking tired, you offer assistance and support at once, and ... help them. Irrespective of the price you must pay.

LUCK. SHEER LUCK – A REAL-LIFE EXAMPLE

It was the same setting (Bosnian War 1992 / 1993) when one of my squad leaders lost a pistol. The night was pitch-dark: An evil night when the Serbs opened fire on everything that moved out there. As 2i/c (second in command; here: 'deputy platoon leader') it was not within my remit to risk my sorry ass and life for the stupidity of my men. When learning of the lost gun (happened right away without any attempt at a cover-up or sugarcoating) I wasted not a single thought on the fact that I could have stayed warm indoors, and safe. It never occurred to me either that I might act on courage (on the contrary: I was scared shitless), but it came to me naturally to immediately start searching for the gun and, ahead of my men, to expose myself to the dangers such a search would entail.

We were lucky. Just lucky.

No one was hit despite heavy machine gun fire all around. And we did find the gun. That mission was important. We should note three things, and it makes no difference what the circumstances are, what area their stage is, be it a family business, a giant corporation, the military or Walmart around the corner. As a leader I had exposed myself to the same dangers as the employees, marched with them shoulder to shoulder, and was a part of them. The action I had initiated met with success. Since my employees had put their cards on the table – prompt report without the attempt of covering it up or sugarcoating – I refrained from pursuing the case afterwards by means of disciplinary proceedings, punishment or reprimand. So, what signals do we leaders hereby send to the employees?

Several!

Being together.

Spontaneity – the leader's singleness of purpose.

The fundamental idea: Honesty pays off.

So why did the squad leader come to me, report to me at once and go out on a limb? Well, because he and his men knew me! The basis for confidence had already been laid, my response was predictable. They knew or sensed how I would react.

Conduct at work impacts success.

In other words: We were successful because my behavior corresponded to their expectations, I did not disappoint them, nor did I counteract these expectations. They trusted me, period. When I had dried off my cold sweat, and when that cold evil night was over, I approached my men as if nothing had ever happened: As we already know, at a distance, authoritarian, full of respect and disciplined!

A FEW EXTRA IMPORTANT ITEMS

Reprimand and Criticism

Should you at some point – and it could happen any day – have to admonish one of your employees, reprimand him or criticize him for his conduct, you will never do so in the presence of others. This is between you and the person before you. No exception! Criticism, no matter how appropriate it might be, is always somewhat degrading. What must never happen is that the employee is stripped of his/her dignity in any way. If somebody believes they have been humiliated, then you will never get close to them again, for you have lost them. You have lost!

How is the Foreign Legion organized?

… or: How do I build my team?

Foreign Legion? Hogwash!

Delete 'Foreign Legion' and replace it by: Lidl, Walmart, Siemens, BASF, Georgs (a gourmet restaurant) or Parts Chain. You should be versatile and convert everything I tell you to fit your purpose. Within your framework, your scheme, your enterprise, your company or your department, etc. They have familiarized you with that absurdity

LEADING, have shown you the ropes, and finally they have let you loose to deal with the gang. With respect, cool distance, without the intimate first-name approach and without that endless shaking of hands, off you go in order to start your work as a role model, authoritarian and disciplined. You may start with the lack of structures or, in case the old pillars should be shaking ominously, you might set about building a team. Your team!

I strongly advise you against the method of railroading things through. Take your time, since your success is at stake, no less. First, you scrutinize your employees, one after another:

- ✓ **Who are these women and men?**

- ✓ **What is their background, their qualification?**

- ✓ **Which of them is best suited for what task (according to their background and qualifications)?**

- ✓ **Who has the potential to assume responsibility, and who absolutely has not?**

Coordinate yourself with the head of HR and think of the future right now.

Increase of the area: Do I perhaps need one or two people who can be in charge?

Gender ratio: Relaxed working could depend on whether I have a good mix of women and men.

Handicaps: Are there any posts for the inclusion of people with a disability/impediment (of the utmost importance!)?

Age: Here, the physical breaking point plays a role, but not exclusively. There are areas of responsibility that call for patience and years of experience. From experience, these are both characteristics of older employees.

THE DEPUTY

Do not hesitate to pick a deputy ASAP.

What should s/he look like?

Looks are not important at all. It is not that important either to choose the most competent one or the one who is everybody's darling. What counts is esprit, not in the sense of acumen or quick-wittedness, rather in the sense of an all-permeating spirit. Select the man or woman who comes closest to your policy, your philosophy and your perception of things. Ideally, this happens to be the spirit and philosophy the company identifies with. And only that makes sense.

Identification with the company!

Should your candidate have any difficulty, replace her/him, go looking for somebody else. Do not tolerate any deviation from the policy in your deputy (except when this deviation is approved by you, when it yields some profit and fosters cooperation).

HOW TO STRUCTURE MY TEAM

Now you structure your team, providing the conditions allow for it. On the team, and you are going to grasp this pretty soon, you have strong as well as weak cadres and employees, but the team itself possesses only so much value, or is only as strong, as its weakest part.

What to do?

To banish the weakest part, to expel it?

Of course not!

The magic word is embedding! We gather round the weakest link in the chain and support it, encourage it, grow it. What we need here is the slogan "Impossible is nothing"; it is our constant companion. Everything is possible at any time, if only everybody wants it!

Everything is possible at any time, if only everybody wants it!

Adopt the following schedule as your own, right from the start. The schedule of clarity. What I mean is that you make sure your employees have everything at their disposal, and I mean everything that they need to meet their tasks and perform under the best imaginable conditions. No one can rattle your cage in that case. If, however, there should be some employees – despite the favorable surroundings, in spite of ideal conditions – who obstruct and work against your credo, then be as tough as nails. Respond with sanctions, if there is no other way, and make sure everybody is getting your message: You are the one who calls the shots!

You call the shots!

Everyone should be aware of that, from the very beginning: Let there be no doubt!

Tough as nails!

Did I say tough as nails?

Let's briefly backtrack to the employee whom you chose as your deputy. S/he has a distinct tendency – and why that is, we probably will never really know for sure – to take over the reins in your absence (vacation or sick leave), in brief: to stage a coup. You are being undermined, your image will be eroded, there is subversion and you will be stabbed in the back. That is not always the case, but it frequently happens. Let's call it envy, lust for power or else. Stupidity is probably the right word. I'm telling you this so that you keep your eyes peeled and are not oblivious to these intrigues. Trust is always a good thing, and, as we know, essential, but don't let your guard down.

Blind faith can end in tragedy.

As a rule: If one of the employees – even if it is your deputy – abuses your trust or is not up to their entrusted duties, since s/he is not up to them, then do not hesitate to demote this staff member to a lower post.

Be: tough as nails!

For yourself.

For him/her.

For everyone.

For joint success!

You will soon realize that there are people among your staff who work autonomously. And they are as trustworthy and reliable as Swiss clockwork, reaching their apogee (efficiency, yield, gain) when you just let them get on with their work. There is nothing they abhor more than when they are under constant and close surveillance. Once they feel that they are being overseen, they clam up, they lose their drive and will end up losing their passion. Then there are others. Of such an ilk that you have to constantly kick their ass. Without a strong authority breathing down their neck, these people are often at a loss. They often won't get really busy unless the boss shows up, but then they will surpass themselves.

For the former, you need gloves of silk. For the latter, crude leather boxing gloves.

It is now your task – which will sometimes mushroom into a real art – to identify the strengths and weaknesses of each and every one, in this respect. Only if you know what makes everybody tick can you forge an efficient and monolithic team from diverse characters. Grind and hone, here and there, smoothing corners and edges!

Have fun … for fun it is anyhow!

GROUP ANALYSIS

A group analysis is one part of team building and its organization, although I consider this term, heavy with meaning (at least in this example), only in relation to the following: What is expected from us as a team or, in other words, to what purpose should each employee (including me) be capable of delivering at any time? I back this question / statement up with an example, so that you understand what I am basically on about. The real-life example: After my time in the Legion, and heavily burdened with all sorts of leadership positions, I accepted a posting with one of the largest German security companies. It was a company that considered itself to be innovative and dynamic. After only four months they put me forward for supervisor, and two months later I got the job. What I saw was a catastrophe, I will come back to it later, but now for the group analysis that I mentioned earlier on. We would work in facilities and branches that could become the target of terrorist attacks at any time. Having read the respective job descriptions, I knew that the profile of an employee had to be as follows:

In top physical condition. Good and impersonal client / customer relations. Good or excellent language proficiency, (English!). Excellent marksman – experienced in the handling of guns. A quicker perception than the average guy.

One day I caught myself scrutinizing my group in that way, and I imagined a few worst-case scenarios – some of the least favorable assumable cases – which could have happened just like that at the time. Well, the company's calculation, wishing to implement security with their staff … it would not have worked out. I only trusted half of the team to be capable of handling their entrusted equipment when going operational. When I say guns, I mainly mean Smith & Wesson, also Taurus 357 Magnum. Hardly any of the men and women could have handled this service weapon so well as to stop a gung-ho assailant with a single aimed shot. Ammunition, nightstick, walkie-talkies, etc. – to most of the employees (and cadres too) these were utensils from another planet. When guarding highly sensitive facilities and institutions, suddenly, I actually did find myself next to former nursery and geriatric nurses, dog parlor owners, conscientious objectors and the long-term unemployed without any relevant previous experience. My initial analysis was that most of these men and women would not withstand the 'first shock' of a well-planned terrorist attack. But that is exactly what they had been hired for. To both the company and the client this was not an ideal situation, far from it, but let us continue: Not even half of the men would have been capable of a 50-meter-sprint to save themselves in time. Only some of them would have managed to carry or drag an injured client out of the danger zone. At most two thirds of the employees had a more or less working knowledge of English. What was striking was the difficulty some of the staff had, even with the German language. The latter is not a value judgment, it is a factual observation. In an emergency – and I knew that from experience, it was not essential to master a language, no matter which one. In an emergency, hands-on experience, perspicacity, a good measure of instinct and great courage were required.

So where was the real problem?

The problem was that nobody was doing anything against the known deficiencies, the lack of training and the prevailing gossip climate. There were no opportunities on offer to keep the staff physically fit. Nobody had in mind to start an in-house language course. The shooting exercises were few and far between, and they were set up in a competitive way or were of a testing nature such that mere statements were made: Bad shooter, good shooter! No one came up with the idea to teach the staff how to handle a gun properly, to lose their fear of it, and how to accurately get a bullet to hit the target ... no one. None of the managers responsible had the idea to put the focus on where it should have been:

- ✓ **Training.**

- ✓ **Further education.**

- ✓ **Professionalism.**

Then, and only then, would mission fulfilment, efficiency and image be ensured.

I was aware of all of this, but I also knew which way the wind blew: What counted was that all positions were filled, and that money was flowing accordingly.

So where is the core message?

The analysis I conducted on my level, regarding my group or my team – is my team up to requirements? – was not done within a superordinate frame, namely for the entire personnel, the company as a whole: Is our company up to requirements?

Nobody asked themselves this question.

Translated into your business, your company or your group: Ask yourself this question. If the bottom line is a NO or a PERHAPS: ... then pull the communication cord! Move heaven and hell for an effective remedy. Say / check where deficiencies are and offer solution concepts, offer your know-how and your spare time. In terms of organization this entails that certain ideas be thought through, and beyond, to arrive at a solution for each problem.

One solution?

For example: An in-house trainer is needed! One who is on top of his subject, a gifted and competent allrounder. Not one you can touch, not one for hugs, but one who brings out maximum efficiency in every person with the aim of preserving the jobs for all, even in the future.

After that there will be no excuses, either.

Not for the boss.

Not for the employee.

In contrast to what I said before, the weak employee is only allowed to 'survive' here, if he shows the will to reach the level of the stronger ones, and that he also possesses their skills, or that he makes every endeavor to acquire them. After all, there are jobs where it is a no-go to embed the weak and pray … *everything will be fine in the end*. Once human lives are at stake, fun and patience must come to an end.

As shift supervisor in the same company, the same district, I once directed the district manager's attention to the high absentee rate due to illness. Needless to say, that it was the young employees in particular, who were prone to be sick, and always when the weather was fine and mostly on the weekend, (we worked 24/7). Funny enough, it was always the same people, too. They were neither profitable for the firm, nor could they be said to perform well. Rather to the contrary. They were grumpy, lazy and they were badmouthing the firm. When I approached the directors in that matter, I got this answer: Yes, there is nothing you can do about it. We cannot lay off anybody who is ill, it is not that simple, and we probably have to put up with it, etc. Well, I begged to differ. It would not do that good employees, who had their weekend off, had to sacrifice this because some colleagues had decided: we call in sick today. This created a bad working atmosphere and it also went to show a certain impotence on behalf of the management. And it was nerve-wrecking (where am I supposed to get three staff members on a Sunday morning at four o'clock, who, preferably of their own volition, would step in and cover for the others?). And it cost money! Most of the staff naturally knew about the state of play, and they would not answer their phones at all when they rang at such ungodly hours.

I decided to take care of the matter.

Mission impossible?

Not at all!

Within a few weeks, I had proven that the call on this or that day … I am ill … did not come from the respective person's home but from a disco. Or I revealed that the person concerned, allegedly lying in agony in their bed at home, played soccer all afternoon with their club, or even that one and the same granny had passed away thrice already, etc., etc. And so, I first achieved that those elements that were damaging the firm, and had only rather insufficiently done their work for a few years, could be dismissed quite legally, and second, that gradually a totally different work culture was setting in. Not one of distrust, but one of …

… we can rely on you!

And this, in turn, empowers the employee – and why not – to claim something. Indignant screams of: here, we are being spied on, they do nasty tricks, use dishonest methods etc., should not prevent a boss from unearthing the truth, and this is what it's all about: Honesty, truth – about trust! He who is beyond reproach can laugh it off and … to hell with the rest! Of course, there's the risk of it getting out of hand. Therefore, take this: No implementation of techniques or procedures that violate data protection, personal integrity or moral ethics. In plain English: No wheeling and dealing!

DEATH TO MULTITASKING

Is there work to be done, does anything need sorting, is there a call for action?

Act promptly!

Do not procrastinate. Execute all the work as soon as it starts coming in. Thereby, you will keep the task- or to-do-list short. You get an email that – regarding the reply – could wait? Reply straight away! And remember: It is not important which tasks you encounter (others will have to decide what's important and unimportant). In the meantime, you should always go to your limits when tackling the tasks – ONE AFTER THE OTHER – and fulfill them par excellence. Make sure you pay utmost attention to your assignments and allocated tasks. There is no such thing as a lower task, nor are there any unimportant assignments. Focus entirely, and with everything at your disposal, on that one task, even if it is just the ordering of toilet paper.

... always get the job done, in total, at once!

But as I have said: one thing after another. Of course, there are priorities. But the trifles that you have not yet dealt with will cloud your view. You excel at multitasking: good for you! But constant multitasking is detrimental. It's the quality of the work that suffers. It exhausts you, you will burn out. At a closer look, multitasking is tantamount to superficiality.

A TEAM LEADER ASKS FOR ADVICE

In the past years, I have been working in the Middle East, in Yemen, to be precise. Trying my mettle as an author, I signed on as an ordinary employee, deliberately waiving the prospect of a leadership position. Time was exactly what I needed to play around with my books as a sideline. (I have always taken a leader's role seriously, and as a boss you do not have any time off – after hours is only in your head). That was working all right for me, I was doing my job like anyone else, however, I would not immerse myself entirely. I lost something along the lines of the eye, the attention. Until one day I found the team leader, almost in despair and in tears, in his office. After a few words he came out with his problems. The team, he thought, was falling apart and he didn't know why. He had no explanation for it. He straightforwardly sought my advice. I spent one week on it, watching what was going on with the eyes of an observant and involved member of staff (and a spy!). When the week was up, I knocked on the team leader's office door. I reported what I had witnessed, and I told him outright what he was doing wrong. For he had actually made some elementary mistakes. Unforgivable, appalling mistakes!

His biggest mistake was the following:

The group consisted of seven employees. Four – amongst them the boss, were from Ireland, one from Scotland, another one from the South of France, and I was from Bavaria. Of course, the Irish employees shared the same interests. They lived near each other, probably had common acquaintances, etc. When off-duty in the evening, they did sports together, to indulge their common ground and – 'we hail from the same neck of the woods' became: we are inseparable friends!

The Scotsman had his own thoughts about it, minded his own business. The guy from the South of France turned up his nose at it. I thought of myself and my books.

It was obvious where the problem was. As a boss – once you have lost the distance to an employee – you cease to be a person of authority. If there are three people patting you on the back, sharing the same playground as you, it's game over for you as a leader or team manager, before it has even started. If you want it or not – it most often happens subconsciously – you cut those three who are from the same neck of the woods as yourself more slack than the others. The benchmark is a different one! To the one you are a friend, to the other you are a leader?

This is doomed to fail!

That was the team leader's first mistake. It was his doing that the team had broken up into three parts (parties).

Another mistake was that, from the beginning, a conspiratorial, inflammatory culture of blathering had developed (and believe me, seven men are worse than a girls' boarding school) and that he had done nothing to stop that. Coffee breaks in particular were used by everyone to criticize in great detail the alleged misconduct of the boss, his preferences for certain staff members, the 'bollox' the personnel department had been hatching, etc. This banter was not done in the open but secretly. As a boss, however, you should have a feel for it.

… an awkward silence sets in as soon as somebody approaches who does not want or should or must not hear this! Or the volume increases, since you want a certain wording to get through to the outside after all (for in spite of all that secrecy you want to be heard anyhow!).

This is common practice in many companies or enterprises, but the problem here was that the team leader himself actively took part in it. He was one of the best when it came to criticizing, sparing none of his employees, not even HR, not to mention the big boss of the corporation, himself. As I said, this was the team leader's second mistake. His third one was to ask questions unbecoming a boss, questions along these lines: I would like to do this or that or I am planning to do this or that ... have you any objections?

Stop!

Lethal trap!

As boss, team leader or supervisor, you are a decision maker.

You take a decision, and it will be executed just like that – period! For later, it is your head on the block, should anything go wrong. The very moment you ask, you give up a piece of your integrity, you reveal a weakness, your authority suffers. There are very specific activities or lines of business where you must or should seek the advice of your employees, ask them before taking a decision, but this is not the rule.

You are a decision maker!

When I told the concerned hapless boss everything, he was flabbergasted. It seemed as if I had held a mirror before his face, in which he saw himself and his mistakes for the first time. My reward was his gratitude! He changed his conduct, kept a distance, refrained from gossiping, but more importantly: he took HIS OWN decisions – and today, he is the epitome of a boss! No one is slapping him on the back anymore.

GRILL YOUR CO-WORKERS!

A little earlier in the text I wrote or asked the following: As a leader, where are the limits of my competencies regarding the domain of HR, admin, etc.? By means of an example I will demonstrate that you, as mentioned, ought to keep out of administrative personnel planning, but that it could be terribly beneficial in that respect, to collaborate tightly with the head of HR – in any case, tighter than some people would like it to be. Namely, when it is about the résumés and the purported qualifications of the employees.

An example from my own experience …

One of my French employees, working with me on behalf of the Delegation of the European Commission, had a brilliant CV (resume, also called Curriculum Vitae). A tad too brilliant for my taste. I could not help but think of the Frenchman to be a fraud, and so I unobtrusively asked him a few questions regarding a particular time span of his professional career, during which, according to his CV, he had been working in a very special position for a reputable firm (Foreign Legion/FL, to call it by its name). I probed into it, pulled my FL strings and lo and behold: This employee had in fact worked for this firm, but only for twenty days – instead of the five years, as he had pretended. Then they kicked him out. It was evident that he had not undergone a proper background check. Private security firms serving the European Commission could not, in theory, afford to have bad apples on their payroll. The risk was just too high. The deplorable reality, however, was a different kettle of fish, entirely, as I had learned. In general, the candidates were subject to strict selection. The selection process for the applicants was not accessible from the outside, yet the RSOs, the mainly responsible security officers, kept a vigilant eye on each and every one of the recently hired. If one of them did not fit the bill – the criteria were stipulated by the RSOs – he fell through the cracks without mercy: Next, please! As a rule, the RSO would interview the candidate individually. It was he who gave the thumbs up. Not necessarily the firm. An RSO who covered different delegations in terms of geography and personnel, usually worked to stringently exact specifications. In that way he was, to a large degree, independent, but he predominantly assumed the role of technical advisor to the different EU-Ambassadors. Besides the consulting of the delegation leaders (ambassadors) in respect of their area of competence regarding dangerous situations, it was also within an RSO's remit to see that appropriate safety measures be observed. He was responsible for the regular conception, the evaluation and the surveillance of a mission. He was responsible for the equipment, the implementation of crucial procedures, and for the safety of people, data and commodities. The whole gamut of his work, however, cannot be defined in a few lines. What I found interesting in this context was a recommendation issued by the organization Human Rights Watch. They contacted oil companies in Columbia in order to contain breaches of human rights. It surely is a bit off-topic, but when taking a closer look, these lines hit the nail on the head. They read: "Diligent examinations of the résumé of former policeman – or army officers who are now private entrepreneurs or employees of security services, should be conducted to ensure that these have not violated human rights or have been members of paramilitary units", (from: War as a Service – Rolf Uesseler, original title and quote in German).

Of course, I did not give a toss why our candidate had been kicked out of the Foreign Legion, in brief: I couldn't care less. What clinched it for him, why I showed him the door without further ado, was the betrayal of confidence. And, as I have said before, confidence is a stone that makes a rock. Trust misplaced, or breach of confidence will cause the rock to crumble, and nobody wants that.

We must underscore the significance of the security officer (read also: HR manager, of a company, responsible for personnel planning and recruitment), as in the end, the success of a company hinges on whether he adheres to his role, or whether he neglects his duties.

N.B.: All companies have safety regulations (see: German/American Occupational Safety and Health Acts; British Factory Act, etc.). What I am on about, however, is especially the safety concerning data protection, internal and external hazards (internal and external offenders), the betrayal of secrets and industrial espionage, sabotage as well as any kind of terrorism.

The employees of bigger corporations or enterprises have been known to harbor economic criminals. A boss should be aware of this.

This is therefore crucial:

- ✓ **The background check.**

- ✓ **The identification.**

- ✓ **The meticulous screening of every applicant's past.**

At a time when quite a lot of people are romping about in our country, who only seem to be controllable, and whose intentions are not always plain obvious, transparency is of the essence. Who wants rotten eggs in their organization?

SUMMARY OF PART 2 OF THE BOOK

Bring out the best in every single employee – jump in at the very deep end for your employees – offer assistance and support – the team is only worth as much or is as strong as its weakest link – definitely banish the word impossible from your vocabulary and facilitate transparency!

THE JOB DESCRIPTION

Real-life example: In mid-1997 a small but exquisite commando operation came about within the framework of a large-scale military mission in sub-Saharan Africa. The aim was to penetrate an enemy-controlled area in the dead of night, to destroy several facilities and to sneak off again. Three small squads infiltrated the area along exactly prescribed paths. There they dealt with their set objective. Evasion (withdrawal or exfiltration) took place along other paths. Every single soldier knew his task. Everything had been meticulously planned, success was preprogrammed. The operation went smoothly, in perfect order. If there had not been …

… one soldier of my squad missing, when we gathered after the brilliant feat!

He did not reach our lines until early morning.

What had happened?

Well, he had not abided by certain procedures. Simple things he should have known, since they were within his brief, things that he had inexcusably chosen to neglect. Although the mission had brilliantly been accomplished in its entirety, I was forced to punish the soldier severely, as in case his non-appearance had lasted a bit longer, other units would have been dispatched to go looking for him, which in turn could have culminated in casualties.

Brief/remit?

That rings a bell!

Sounds like job description, which again sounds like alphabet soup. But this is where we are wrong. Everything is simple if only you take the easy way. Job description, in simple terms, determines who does what, when, with what means and with whom.

… who does what, when, with what means and with whom?

Job descriptions restrict the tasks and competencies that go with the respective job, and they do so concisely and clearly, and that is how they have to be understood: Setting limits – where do the employee's competencies begin and where do they end. Such a job description should not be sophisticated and rigid in its application, but simple, neat and above all flexible. Flexible in the sense of … free of deadlines: In fact, something that, in the course of weeks, months or years, can be altered at short notice, at the drop of a hat, or be adjusted to a novel field of duties. If an employee is outside the set limits, if s/he falls short or transgresses them, then it is time for action.

Time for action may take the form of 'punishment'. In plain English: a verbal scolding, a disciplinary warning, etc.

What is the Foreign Legion's take on that?

In the Legion a mistake entails immediate punishment. This is often fierce. But with it, the file is closed: once and for all. No repeated chicanery will result from it, you do not talk about it anymore, it is water under the bridge! That's how I learned it. I didn't do it differently, myself. Do not let the staff member atone for the mistake that he made umpteen weeks ago. He took responsibility for it, all have learned their lesson. If, however, the same mistake enters a second round …!

You know my slogan: Be tough as nails! After all, the warning had been issued.

A job description conveniently begins with an organigram, so that the employee schematically sees his place in the company. It is a structure that, at one glance, demonstrates where the person concerned is within the company. Here are some points that are important, but they will differ from company to company, such as:

Job title.

Immediate superiors.

Proxy.

Subordinate positions – goal of the position / the post.

Working hours, (framework agreements / others).

Scope, (tasks and competencies) etc.

A job description is like a challenge, a performance expectation by the bosses for the employee, but one in which, if possible, the person concerned participates. But, as I said, the framework should be kept as flexible as possible, yet without leaving room for doubt.

… who does what, when, with what means and with whom?

Keep it short and simple when devising a job description. It is a matter of saying everything with few words on paper, and take care that everything that is on it is in unison with what the employment contract already specifies. Sometimes you come across corporate job descriptions that are nothing but closed books concerning both length and gobbledygook. Please: Keep it short and simple and leave no space for misinterpretation.

When varying the tasks / fields of duties, it can be useful to appoint a coordinator who attends to the matter.

THE GOLDEN MEAN

To find it is probably the most difficult task for a supervisor, team leader, district- or department head. You want, and you have to please the superior whose trust you enjoy, and you must or should not fall out with the subordinate employees.

To start off: You may well try to please everyone … and you will find that you yourself fall by the wayside!

We know – to please everyone is an art no one can master (German proverb)! As a basic rule: The management cannot always have their way. The big bosses in the airconditioned offices often do not know what it is like in the lower echelons, where the everyday winds are blowing. It is the team leaders' role to constantly remind the executive floor of this daily routine or to open their eyes to it. To do so requires courage and some diplomacy. If it is right to behave at a distance, in an authoritarian way, with respect – top-down – it is also advisable to display the same attitude bottom-up. It probably is advisable to hold back a little regarding the authoritarian posture here. Still: When dealing with the leadership, don't be a wimp. You also hold a leadership position. As soon as the upper rank of leadership wants to introduce something new, something innovative, as soon as they plan on changes, want new work processes, job cuts or, on the contrary, they envisage additional posts in your area, and you know or feel that these changes can only go wrong:

You say so!

For the sake of God, do not be a yes-man on principle!

Put your objections forward.

Give your point of view, unequivocally.

Get behind your crew and protect them (there are of course situations when you cannot protect anyone) and make your mark.

... the boss backs us to the hilt!

I have been searching my long active time in the Legion for some examples. Of course, I came up with a few finds, but the best example is from a book on legionnaires in the Indochina War. I am talking about France's Foreign Sons by Paul Bonnecarrère (original title in German). Here is my version. It is a quite amusing but authentic story that I have shortened, using my own words, as it is too elaborate in the book. The whole thing happened in Saigon in June 1946. A legionnaire, who was prone to drinking and who frequently embarked on pub crawls at night in between battles, reported one morning to his company commander, sporting a black eye. He told him that the previous evening he had been with a girl. Unfortunately, her boyfriend, a colonel of the regular army, returned home earlier than planned and caught the two red-handed. The colonel dealt the legionnaire a blow to the eye, but the latter punched back and sent the officer to the land of Nod. Now the colonel came to the company commander, complaining, and demanding a punishment – a court martial, no less. To this end, the company commander was meant to have his company fall in the following morning to identify the legionnaire by his black eye, and to have him arrested. What did the company commander do?

Correct!

Within the hour he has the company on roll call (about 100 men) and he orders that everyone should deal his next buddy a black eye, and vice versa. When the colonel appeared, accompanied by the police, there were 100 men in front of him, all with a black eye; hence, an identification had become impossible.

What does that mean for us, here and now? Well, the boss had protected his employee. Dirty linen is washed within the family. That is the core message. Now it is your turn to transfer such an example to your area – but please, no shiner!

THE CODE OF HONOR

Ever thought about it? The Legion has a code of honor which accompanies the legionnaire's entire life (… and far beyond that!). In seven short articles, and in few words (in fact, there are only 158 words) a guideline on personal conduct is offered, and everybody is eager to follow it. But as I have said before: Legion? Hogwash! We need team rules instead of the code of honor.

… although they both amount to just about the same.

For the common denominator is that both – code or rule – stipulate a course of conduct with which everybody likes to identify. Behavior like the following:

Suggestions and ideas are judged on the grounds of their objective contents and their factual applicability, and not by their author's position.

Every employee has the right to talk with everyone about everything, all of which contributes to the implementation of a common task.

Collective well-being trumps individual well-being.

It is a duty to hear the other one out, always.

You cannot grant anybody a wish, if the wish is not verbalized.

It is a duty to think aloud, any judgments are forbidden.

Anyone who gets caught badmouthing an employee, puts money in the kitty.

We all make mistakes. But it is everybody's duty to correct identified mistakes and to prevent their repetition.

Nobody has the right to criticize or boycott joint decisions once they have been taken.

An idea is neither wrong nor right!

As a basic rule: Every person is entitled to clearly speak his/her mind or to voice their concerns.

These rules are merely a guideline. And if these were rules that had been made together? Summon your team as fast as possible, set up your team rules, and ...

... did anyone in the audience say that it would be a bad idea to fix those rules on a big sheet of paper, framed perhaps, to the wall or hang it above the door or at a spot that everyone has to pass at least once in the course of day? Funny descriptions, nicely done up – to be taken seriously!

THAT GUY IS TAKING IT TOO FAR

Among other things, there is one item in the Foreign Legion's code of honor, which is of utmost importance: 'Every Legionnaire is your brother-at-arms, irrespective of his nationality, race or creed. You will demonstrate this by an unwavering and straightforward solidarity which must always bind together members of the same family'. I know what you are thinking: The guy is taking it too far! Lidl, BASF, Siemens and Walmart (or BMW and Home Depot) are not the Foreign Legion. And I tell you: You are wrong (a bit). Because here it is not about: Who is busy or preoccupied where with whom and in which context or in what circumstances, but it is about the contents, about values and honesty. I am talking about marginalization, about mobbing and acceptance. Everyone, every single person in your department must feel comfortable, everybody deserves their chance – without distinction. Therefore: Be alert. As soon as you gain knowledge of employees being teased, mobbed or ostracized – no matter why –, you take uncompromising action, you make your mark.

NOT HERE – NOT WITH US

NOT TODAY – NOT TOMORROW

And to use big words: The dignity of each human being is inviolable!

SUMMARY OF PART 3 OF THE BOOK

You must make sure that everybody knows: … who does what, when, with what means and with whom? Where do the employee's competencies begin, where do they end? Keep it simple. The shorter, the better! This goes for anything in writing. Short, simple and accurate. If an employee is outside the set limits, if s/he falls short or transgresses them, then it is time for action. In case of a repeated disregard of your instructions, then: Be tough as nails! Don't be a wimp! Dirty laundry is washed within the family. Everybody deserves their chance. Be alert. It is about the contents, values and honesty. The dignity of each human being is inviolable!

THE BEST RESULTS?

You achieve the best results by repeating your instructions or intentions, over and over and again, at every imaginable occasion. Over time, a form of automatism will set in. This might be annoying, but it is memorable. Have you any doubt that your instructions might have been taken on board? So, repeat them. Make inquiries. Turn up on everybody's doorstep. Let me be bold and claim that behavior at work – positive thinking – punctuality – discipline – reliability and professionalism – impacts success in every respect. All of these features can be acquired. Add a healthy portion of common sense, and they will inevitably lead to success. Make sure a good performance is appreciated AND take care that the employee knows that you know whenever good work is done. In order to achieve best results, you as a superior are first and foremost called upon. Show yourself. Demonstrate to your employees that you have an interest in the cause. Be omnipresent. Check, control, get on people's nerves!

Be happy when everything is running the way you want it and show your delight. Be angry if this is not the case and show your anger.

Be hot and be cold ... but never lukewarm. Enhancement of performance and transgression of boundaries through motivation.

WHAT IS MOTIVATION?

Fancy a success story? In the spring of 1989, I was caporal (PFC – private first class), and was summoned to the regimental commander. My transfer to the NCO training course in the south of France was imminent. A caporal has been summoned to the regimental commander? If you are not a legionnaire, it is hard to fathom what that means. It had an I-am-not-sleeping-for-three-weeks-to-come-effect! To us, the colonel was a sort of demigod. A demigod you would only see from a great distance, who only had to look at us to make us storm the enemy's bastions, cheering, disregarding our own casualties, but this only in passing. Contrary to my expectations, I did not drop dead upon entering the colonel's office. After a rather uptight presentation, I hardly believed my eyes. The colonel circled his desk, ordered "at ease", smiled amiably at me and ... extended his hand.

For ten whole minutes he was talking to me as if I were the most important person on earth, and if anything else could wait. He told me what to expect from the course and he also said that he wished for me to invest all my energy and to be a best seller there:

In the name of his regiment (the company)!

For our common cause!

He also hinted at the fact that, should I pass the course well, I would immediately be deployed as a squad leader.

After he had bid me farewell, not without wishing me success, yet again, I left the office. My feet were hardly touching the floor, I was on cloud nine. This feeling of a liftoff would last fifteen years. The colonel had managed, with a few words, to convince me that I was a tremendously important building block in his enterprise (which comprised 1,300 building blocks), but more importantly: I believed every single word he said. His demeanor, his language, his whole aplomb: It was all authentic. There was nothing coerced, nothing gave the impression of being phony. Motivated to the highest degree, I successfully passed the training course as the second-best out of fifty-five candidates.

OK – I know! It was I, no less, who wrote that a boss should not necessarily shake hands, but here it's different. The level is a totally different one, with the colonel as the big chief executive and me but a small aspiring head of department, and that changes everything.

During those ten minutes of our casual conversation, I very quickly grasped the essence (that I would do so, the colonel knew too!). The gist was the following:

Our enterprise is unique, it is among the best, it is successful.

You are an important part of it.

Invest yourself entirely for the benefit of your enterprise.

If you meet with success, this will contribute to the enhancement of our image.

Excel, and I shall guarantee: It will be rewarded!

This is pure motivation!

Now: What is keeping you, as team leader, head of department, supervisor or shift manager, from having an appointment with the big boss? Just ask! State some trivial reason for seeing him, one that seems sufficiently important. And when you finally stand in front of the boss, you ask him, if it were possible for him to come to your department one day, to briefly meet each of your (his) employees in person. Tell him forthright that your employees' motivation would increase enormously, if the big boss himself appeared to call everyone by their name and, for a change, to spare five or ten minutes for a small chat. If he should refuse, and this is the worst that could happen to you, this is not a big deal. But keep in mind that the big boss is anything but a fool. He will memorize your name (it does not happen every day that such a scamp walks through the door, not to mention with such an outrageous request), since privately, he thinks your idea is good. Should he decline, then it is most likely that his plate is rather full. But he is going to carry your idea with him, and he will think about it, should your paths cross one day.

If, however, you are successful, and the boss really makes an appearance, your department is prone to be talking about this moment for years to come. Brownie points for you ... you will be admired for your bravery -, brownie points for your department.

LEAD YOUR TEAM INTO THE CHAMPIONS' LEAGUE

If you manage, as an executive, to foster a sense of togetherness, and if this sense evolves into a kind of pride: Proud to have the privilege of working here, you will lead one-nil. If you then express during a personal talk with every single one of your employees how essential their individual contribution is for the company, then you will be the match winner, and if you take it one step further and ask of every single person to always commit themselves 100 per cent, to also identify 100 per cent with the company, then you have secured your place in the champions' league. If you want to motivate, it would be favorable to know what demotivates. Generate a list yourself about what has demotivated you when you held the same or a similar position as your employees at the moment. Would it read like that?

- **Boredom, always the same daily routine, the same processes and the same faces.**

- **Fixed salary and not a chance – no matter if you perform 100 per cent or just half – to see it increased. No profit-sharing.**

- **Superiors who are not motivated.**

- **Always to sit or to stand up, short breaks or none at all.**

- **Task or target not clearly defined, and if they are, the benchmark is so high that task and target cannot be reached.**

- **Hardly any praise. No one sees my faculties.**

- **Work is no fun.**

The list can be quite long. Shorten it! Work on eliminating as many demotivating factors as possible, once and for all, and above all: Break through the daily routine that is creeping through the factory halls and office premises like a curse! How? Why don't you do something crazy?! Something that nobody does because it is daring, out of the ordinary, something that is ... simply different. What? Have you no imagination? When you reply, here and now, with a No, hand back your leadership commission!

DELEGATING: AN ART THAT ISN'T AN ART!

A small success story: On July 25, 1995 a handmade bomb, spiked with nasty metal splinters, went off on a Parisian suburban train at the station Saint-Michel Notre-Dame. The explosion killed eight people and injured more than one hundred. Fast, it became clear that this was a terrorists' act. Under the Anti-Terror Bill, the Foreign Legion was also deployed to maintain peace and order and to avert further perils. To deploy the Army, and especially the Legion, to preserve public order and internal/homeland security was a strong signal sent by President Chirac. For us legionnaires, the time had come to leave all our cares behind after the perturbing fights in Africa and in the Balkans. As a sergent-chef, I oversaw the deployment of several small teams. Each team consisted of three men, and it was to be accompanied by one gendarme. According to my company commander, the task was extremely important, so do not make any mistakes. All perfect, that was his claim. Heavily armed, we were to patrol the murky passageways of the Metro and the commuter trains in Paris, day and night. Time was scarce, as we had been informed at short notice, and were meant to leap into action upon arrival. In less than two hours we had to move into the allocated accommodations. The entire specific material should be taken over from the predecessors. It was imperative to contact the gendarmes and the civil organizations as fast as possible. At the same time, preferably. Before our teams were dispatched for the first time, I held a briefing in my Metro headquarters with all participants present. In front of the assembled company I detailed the mission order from A to Z. The last word had hardly been spoken, and the last question answered, when my sergeants distributed the weapons. They equipped the legionnaires with flashlights, night sticks, handcuffs, ammunition and various other security-related gadgets. Metro timetables were handed to the team leaders who accepted maps, checked the walkie-talkies, received details on the relief points and on the scheduled reliefs. And of course, we engraved on each soldier's forehead every last guideline pertaining to the use of force, similar to the rules of engagement. As the teams were spreading out, I was not the only one to know: Paris would be sleeping well that night! All the teams were on the move. And myself? I for my part was dead on my feet, I was too tired to personally find out if our first mission had started off successfully. I was virtually asleep standing upright, almost incapable of thinking clearly anymore – I was running on empty!

… and I began to think.

What had happened?

Where had I gone wrong?

I was too close, and I had lost the plot!

I had coordinated, given orders and organized things, I wanted to be everywhere at the same time, and I would have preferred to take everything into my own hands, but there would have been an easier way for me. Not only easier, but also more efficient – meaning, with so much more remaining energy that I could have pursued my role as global head of operations better, even after the mission had kicked off. The following day, I had brought the briefing forward by an hour, and I had only summoned the sergeants and PFCs – in brief: the team leaders. I gave each of them the orders in writing, announced key times and then I reclined and relaxed. What happened was exactly what I had been hoping for, exactly what I had expected. The team leaders were looking at me in disbelief. When they realized that they had carte blanche, this felt like a liberation. They gathered their teams, full of vigor, and they set about their job with enthusiasm, while I was doing my work, able to make plans for the following days. All I had to do was run random checks on whether my instructions were being executed to a T and fully understood the way I had given them.

The slips of paper with the instructions only contained the essential – as we already know: Who does what, when, with what means!

The first positive effect incurred by my measure was that I – although I was totally snowed under – finally had more time and I stayed on top of things. The core message and the lessons that I had learned?

I had delegated – assigned responsibility. I had given my trust and been paid back in excellent work.

By delegating, I made space for other important things, I distributed the workload, thereby reducing my own stress level.

I could preoccupy myself with, for example: What happens, if …! I was able to plan ahead.

To the young leaders whom I hardly knew, it was a test. They could prove their mettle and soak up a bit of what is called self-confidence. They virtually grew with their task, were entirely taken up in it.

I had – and that was the most precious discovery – ascertained … that it works without me!

Motivate your team by delegating and by passing on information and know-how. Contrary to common belief, delegating is not an art, all it requires is a bit of courage and a certain amount of logic, and above all – do not come up with a fifty-five-items plan, but keep it simple.

Who does what, when, with what means!

BATTERIES EMPTY?

You are hyper, your batteries are always full, but you also know from experience that these can empty very quickly, and then it's Good night, Vienna. Therefore: Relax whenever you have the opportunity. Use any option to recharge your batteries.

- You are entitled to a lunch break? **Don't waive it!**

- Ten minutes between two things? **Relax!**

And if there was a quiet place where you could sleep for 20 minutes? Or just doze off? As a leader, you must be awake, on the spot mentally, physically fit (according to your possibilities) and up to scratch intellectually. As a person in charge, and subject to the high demands, the stress and the expectations of the higher echelons, you are always face-to-face with the burnout, except: You do not give the burnout a chance, burnout is not in your dictionary!

Why?

Very simple!

Let me tell you that burnout is a great danger. We know that a danger that we know is no longer a danger. Simple, isn't it? If you observe the following items, you will soon notice that these are not just words.

- ✓ Keep physically fit. Go running three times a week and burnout can kiss your a.. .

- ✓ Have a laugh as often as possible.

- ✓ Do not take yourself sooooo seriously.

Anything goes wrong? So what! Neither your boss nor you nor your employees are perfect. Even the gods make mistakes!

Do not bring any work home. Do not (if possible) work on ninety-six projects simultaneously. Step by step! You have one or more projects, one or more tasks, you are working on them – you have ultimate success? Hooray! And only then it's time to tackle the next challenges.

And once again, as I am being very serious, and as it is of vast importance:

Smile!

Something went wrong?

Smile!

As Shakespeare once put it: 'Wise men ne'er sit and wail their loss, but cheerly seek how to redress their harms'.

What is essential is that at home (ideally amongst your family) you find stability. Discuss your problems with your partner. Get your suffering off your chest – man, that's good! Talk to the neighbor, to friends … to your lover! If these are not listening, they are the wrong friends, crap neighbors and lovers you may forget about.

Quite often, it happens that you – especially as an executive – get battered like a leaf in the autumn wind. People who work in the social sector are particularly exposed. Professional and human demands are often very high, and a lot of resilience, flexibility and sensitivity is required.

To you as an executive it is imperative: Do not bottle everything up! You have an account. There is strength in it. Withdraw some of it every day – and soon it will be depleted, you go down. What is important here: Talk, talk at all costs. One thing is certain – brooding makes you sick!

Brooding is like rats nibbling at your soul!

There are people who go home, bottle everything up, they are mute, alone. Many of these human beings (… more than you might think) take to the bottle, are searching for motivation in the booze. You will not do that, since you are a real executive and above such things, for you observe all these points:

1. To discuss problems and difficult moments.

2. To strike a balance.

3. To laugh.

4. Simply to relax, go hiking, craft your children's future together with them, make paper airplanes, catch butterflies and color them, pull clowns by their nose.

5. To cry. Yes … have a ball crying tears.

6. To dare discuss with superiors all those things that burden you.

7. To train for a half-marathon next year (… or for a game of cards with friends at the weekend).

8. To have dreams. Oh yes! You dream of a better world, and it brightens up your beautiful face.

SUMMARY OF PART 4 OF THE BOOK

Break the daily routine in your department. If you lack the imagination to do something out of the ordinary, return your leadership commission. Simply learn to delegate: Who does what, when, with what means. Learn to relax. Lead your team into the champions' league … not the district league! Brooding is like rats nibbling at your soul! Replenish your strength-account by talking, laughing, crying and making amends.

LIDL, WALMART, H&M AND CHARISMA

Before finishing this book, I had nothing more stupid to do than spend the weeks shopping as an ordinary customer in the numerous small and medium-sized company stores. Every time I met an employee, no matter if at Lidl, Walmart, H&M, Kaufland or Mediamarkt (the latter two are typically German retailers), if at the cash desk or in the men's department, I would ask – rather directly –: "What motivates you most in your work?" If they hesitated for more than three seconds, I would up the ante at once.

"How happy are you with your boss?"

Almost 100 per cent of the men and women had a timid smile in their face, they turned their eyes to the left as a precaution, then back to the right and then back to the left (just as if they were crossing a street), and then, recalcitrant and a bit subdued they would say.

"I'd rather not comment on that!"

There you go! An answer could not be any more definite. So, here is my advice:

Get to work, you who wish to be leaders, or …

… serve a one-year apprenticeship in the Foreign Legion!

Finally, what are those leadership qualities? I have been avoiding this question deliberately, thus far. For that simple reason. There are a thousand qualities a leader must or can have. There is no unanimity, and there is always the one to correct and point out something better. If you are to ask me, however, how I personally picture my / a boss, then the answer is simple.

A leader is somebody who is where he is because he has prevailed against the masses. He has got the clout! He is someone who looks impressive, who gets things straight and who is good to his word! He never lies! Someone who does not kiss up and kick down.

Somebody who, every time I see him, makes me blush because he is simply better than me at everything, and who, when he's talking, commands the silence in the audience for everybody is listening.

This is what you call CHARISMA.

Philip Rosenthal once said: "Success in life is a little substance, a little semblance and an awful lot of close shaves." (Original quote in German). This may well apply to success in general. If, however, it is all about successful leadership, you can safely rest assured that you will need a little luck and one hell of a lot of substance.